Presented to

From

Date

Let this be for you an encouragement, that with all diligence and earnestness it may become your habit to pray. For next to the preaching of the Gospel, in which God speaks with us and gives us all His grace and blessings, the highest and foremost work we can do is to speak with Him through prayer and receive from Him what He gives us. We have this great need of prayer, for by it we are truly able to keep what we have and to defend it against our enemies—the devil and the world. By our prayer we seek and find what we are to receive. Therefore prayer becomes our comfort, strength, and consolation, as well as our protection against all enemies and our victory over them.

—Martin Luther
Exposition of John 16:23, 1537

Lutheran
BOOK *of* PRAYER

CONCORDIA PUBLISHING HOUSE · SAINT LOUIS

3558 South Jefferson Avenue, Saint Louis, Missouri 63118-3968
1-800-325-3040 • cph.org

Compiled and edited by Scot A. Kinnaman.

Original prayers and revisions of prayers from previous editions contributed by Randy Asburry, Robert C. Baker, Peter Cage, William Cwirla, Julene Dumit, Daniel Gard, Deborah Henry, Clarence Hinz, Dean Kavouras, Scot A. Kinnaman, Laura L. Lane, Paul T. McCain, Christopher Mitchell, Pamela Nielsen, John Pless, Rodney Rathmann, Steven J. Resner, Stephen Rosebrock, Mark Sell, Walter Snyder, Walter Steele, D. Rick Stuckwisch, and John Wohlrabe, for Concordia Publishing House.

Other prayers and devotional material adapted from the following: *Gebets-Schatz (Evangelical Lutheran Treasury of Prayers)*, copyright © 1894 and 1899 Concordia Publishing House, translated by Charles Schaum; *Family Prayers*, copyright © 1930 Concordia Publishing House; *Daily Prayers*, copyright © 1935 Concordia Publishing House; *Treasury of Prayers*, copyright © 1956 Concordia Publishing House.

Except for Scripture quotations in quotations of Luther's Small Catechism, Scripture quotations are from The Holy Bible, English Standard Version, copyright © 2001 by Crossway, a division of Good News Publishers. Used by permission. All rights reserved.

Scripture quotations in quotations of Luther's Small Catechism are from the HOLY BIBLE, NEW INTERNATIONAL VERSION®. NIV®. Copyright © 1973, 1978, 1984 by International Bible Society. Used by permission of Zondervan Publishing House. All rights reserved.

The Small Catechism quotations are from *Luther's Small Catechism with Explanation*, copyright © 1986, 1991 Concordia Publishing House. All rights reserved.

Hymn stanzas and canticles marked with the abbreviation *LSB* are from *Lutheran Service Book*, copyright © 2006 Concordia Publishing House.

Manufactured in China

1 2 3 4 5 6 7 8 9 10 34 33 32 31 30 29 28 27 26 25

Contents

Preface

This new edition of *Lutheran Book of Prayer* is issued with the conviction that prayers of Christians are not futile gestures or mere pious exercises, but mighty means by which we call upon God for help and strength for the various needs of faith and life. The words of promise "Call upon Me in the day of trouble; I will deliver you, and you shall glorify Me" (Psalm 50:15) are one of the foundation stones on which this work is based.

This collection of prayers is not published with the design of curtailing or stifling the praises and petitions that Christians formulate when they appear before God. Rather, it is intended to stimulate and aid such praying and to assist believers in making their whole life one of communion with the Father in heaven. Many Christians, when meditating on the situation in which they are placed, desire to have some thoughts, words, and phrases suggested in which their inmost longing can become definite and articulate. To meet such desires these prayers are offered.

This edition again includes a selection of psalms not only to place some of these divine gems directly into your hands but also to draw attention to the prayer book of the Holy Scriptures, with which no child of God can become too familiar. Luther's Small Catechism is included in the hope that its constant prayerful perusal will keep alive in you the intimate acquaintance with the basic Christian truths that all disciples of Jesus desire to possess.

This new edition reflects the long tradition of *Lutheran Book of Prayer* and draws strongly on the prayers, resources, and topics seen from the earliest editions. Also included here for the first time are several newly written prayers as well as prayers and devotions freshly translated and adapted from a variety of beloved Lutheran prayer books from previous generations.

It is the publisher's hope that all who use this *Lutheran Book of Prayer* will find fulfilled for themselves the Savior's gracious promise "Ask, and it will be given to you; seek, and you will find; knock, and it will be opened to you" (Matthew 7:7).

GOD'S COMMAND AND PROMISE REGARDING PRAYER

Dear Lord! You know that I cannot come before You on account of my own self, my presumption or my worthiness. Just as I might desire to look upon You, yet in the same way I would not be permitted to do so and would not even know how I might begin to pray. Nevertheless I do come before You because You Yourself have commanded it and You earnestly encourage that we should call upon You. You have even pledged a promise. You sent Your own Son, He who teaches us what we should pray, and You have promised to give us the words that we use in prayer. Therefore I know that such prayer indeed pleases You, and that my claim, that I may commend myself as a child of God before You, as great as that may seem, comes from the fact that I must obey You as You would have it. May I never inflict lies upon You and through other and greater sins trespass against You, thereby despising Your command and rejecting the gift of faith in Your promise. (1)

—Martin Luther

Prayers
for
MORNING & EVENING

General Prayer

FOR MORNING*

In the name of the Father and of the Son and of the Holy Spirit. Amen.

I thank You, my heavenly Father, through Jesus Christ, Your dear Son, that You have kept me this night from all harm and danger; and I pray that You would keep me this day also from sin and every evil, that all my doings and life may please You. For into Your hands I commend myself, my body and soul, and all things. Let Your holy angel be with me, that the evil foe may have no power over me. Amen. (2)

—Martin Luther

Let each day begin with prayer,
Praise, and adoration.
On the Lord cast ev'ry care;
He is your salvation.
Morning, evening, and at night
Jesus will be near you,
Save you from the tempter's might,
With His presence cheer you.
(*LSB* 869:2)

General Prayer

FOR EVENING*

In the name of the Father and of the Son and of the Holy Spirit. Amen.

I thank You, my heavenly Father, through Jesus Christ, Your dear Son, that You have graciously kept me this day; and I pray that You would forgive me all my sins where I have done wrong, and graciously keep me this night. For into Your hands I commend myself, my body and soul, and all things. Let Your holy angel be with me, that the evil foe may have no power over me. Amen. (3)

—Martin Luther

My loved ones, rest securely,
For God this night will surely
From peril guard your heads.
Sweet slumbers may He send you
And bid His hosts attend you
And through the night watch o'er your beds.
(*LSB* 880:5)

*From Luther's Small Catechism.

Sunday

MORNING

Lord God, You are the Almighty One who fills all eternity and whose name is holy. Yet You have assured us that You dwell with each baptized believer in Christ. On this first day of the week, I pray that all who hear Your holy Word would experience the fulfillment of that promise.

By Your holy Gospel enter my heart and make it Your own dwelling place. As Your holy Word is being preached and Your holy Sacraments given to me, let me receive Your grace with a believing heart, that being so strengthened I may be not only a hearer of Your Word, but also a doer of Your will to my neighbor.

Restore unto me the joy of Your salvation and give me the strength to put into practice what I have heard and confessed. Keep me a humble learner for as many days as You give me on earth, and then receive me into the heavenly home You have prepared for me; through Jesus Christ, Your Son, our Redeemer. Amen. (4)

Sunday

EVENING

I thank You, O Father, Lord of heaven and earth, that You have again revealed to us Your grace and forgiveness in Christ Jesus by the preaching of Your holy Gospel. Bless Your Word everywhere it has been proclaimed, and let it be the power of salvation to all who have heard it. Open the eyes of those who are still blind and do not know You as the only true God or Your Son, Jesus Christ, whom You have sent. Send out Your light and Your truth to all who are without Christ, without God, without hope in this world, and lead them also to the knowledge of Your glory in the face of Jesus.

Forgive my sins for the sake of Your Son, my Redeemer, Jesus Christ. Let Your Word be a constant comfort in life and death. Let it guide me wherever I go, let it cheer me as I prepare for sleep, let me be mindful of it when I get up, so that, as I live, I live in You, and whenever I die, I die in You. Therefore, whether I live or die, I am Your own beloved child. Amen. (5)

Monday

MORNING

Lord, in this morning hour I come boldly to Your throne of grace in full assurance that there I shall obtain mercy and find grace and help in time of trouble. I need Your help and Your grace as I again return to the routine of my vocation and schedule. Grant me true faithfulness in the performance of my calling. Guard me against becoming selfish, careless, and lazy in carrying out my daily work, so that all I do has not only the appearance of being pleasing among men, but is also true service to my neighbor, that I may be a servant of Christ, doing the will of God.

Grant to all who are out of work useful employment. Feed us all with food necessary for our lives, and teach us to receive it with thanksgiving. Grant us the godliness and contentment without which there can be no true happiness, and let us so walk through the things temporal that we may not lose the things eternal; for Jesus' sake. Amen. (6)

Monday

EVENING

Lord, You have searched me and You know me! You know when I sit down and when I stand up; even from a distance You know my very thoughts. You know what I have put my hands to during the day and the content of my dreams at night. You are acquainted with all my ways. Alas, You know also how often I have sinned against You this day, how often I have transgressed Your holy Law, and how often I have failed to keep my promises of loyalty to You and Your Word. Lord do not enter into judgment against Your servant. Do not deal with me in accordance with my sin, and do not give me the just reward for my iniquities, but rather graciously blot out all my trespasses for the sake of Your own Son, in whose blood I have redemption and the forgiveness of sins. As the night darkens around me, I again come to You for Your gracious protection, firmly trusting that You will keep Your child safe from all danger of body and soul. Grant to me and all Your children refreshing sleep, so that with renewed energy we may awake to serve You in our daily vocation; in Jesus' name. Amen. (7)

Tuesday

MORNING

In Holy Baptism, O triune God, You entered into my heart and made it Your temple and dwelling-place. Keep me always mindful of this high distinction. Whenever Satan seeks to seduce me to sin, to neglect Your Word and will, to dishonesty, selfishness, and envy, help me to resist him in Your strength, to beat back his attacks and obtain the victory. Father in heaven, let me never forget that I am Your child and that Satan's only purpose is to separate me from You. O Savior, Jesus Christ, keep Your bitter suffering ever before me, so that I hate and abhor every sin, no matter how small it may seem. O Holy Spirit, who has regenerated me, keep me in this newness of life, and let not Satan lure me back into the way that leads to eternal damnation. Triune God, keep me constant in Your means of grace—the Word and Sacraments—that in the power of Your might I may be able to withstand in the evil day and, having done all, to stand. Hear me for Jesus' sake. Amen. (8)

Tuesday

EVENING

Almighty God, Ruler of heaven and earth, I thank You that You have preserved me from sickness and misfortune, from dishonor and shame, from famine and starvation, from hunger and thirst. You have given me food according to my need. You have granted me life, and in Your mercy You have blessed my life and preserved my spirit. Oh, give thanks to the Lord for He is good, and His mercy endures forever. Lord, in this evening hour I come to You, confessing my many transgressions committed during the day. I am ashamed and blush to lift my face to You, O God. Yet trusting in the atoning sacrifice of Your Son, I ask You to forgive all my sins and to cover them with the righteousness of Jesus, our Savior, so that though they be as scarlet, they shall be white as snow. I come to You for Your continued protection this night and all the days of my life, until I arrive at the land where there is no night but everlasting day in the glory of Your presence. Hear me for the sake of my Redeemer, Your Son, Jesus Christ. Amen. (9)

Wednesday

MORNING

Lord Jesus, You have chosen me out of the world to be Your own in time and in eternity. Though I am no longer of the world, You have not yet taken me out of this earthly tent into my eternal home. I am still in this world surrounded by dangers I cannot begin to number and exposed constantly to temptation. Let me never forget that this world will end with all its evil pleasures and only those who do the will of God will abide forever. Increase and preserve in me that faith in You and in Your redeeming work which is the victory that overcomes the world. Give me that fervent love that would not think of choosing the things of this world—its riches, its glories, and its pleasures—and on their account forgetting You and Your salvation. Teach me to despise the world's mockery, its hatred, and its threats, knowing that even if it should succeed in depriving me of some advantage in this life, it can never rob me of You and Your promise of life forever at Your side. While I yet travel through life, preserve me in the faith that claimed me as a child of Your heavenly household, until that time when You would receive me into my heavenly home. Amen. (10)

Wednesday

EVENING

Dear Savior, You have brought me safely to the end of this day. I did not know Your plan for me—what troubles and what joys would be part of my day; and now the day is done. Lord, grant that I may look back at all the things that You provided and recognize the good You have done for me. Let me view the successes of the day as encouragements and as undeserved gifts coming from Your gracious hands. Let me accept the pains and perplexities as reminders, chastening, and directions toward repentance and improvement. The day has gone, O Savior, and I am closer to the hour when I shall see You face-to-face. Let this passing of time make me more ready and watchful for the hour when You will come. Let me more eagerly prepare myself for that day. O Lord, it is better to depart this life and be with You; wash me in Your blood that I can stand before You. But if You would keep me here, then let me be steadfast in faith, abundant in service, warm in love, and unceasing in prayer. You have redeemed me, my great God and Savior; I am Yours. Amen. (11)

Thursday

MORNING

Lord Jesus, by Your regenerating grace given in Baptism, You have made me a new creature through Your redeeming blood. I confess to You, Searcher of hearts, that in me also, that is in my sinful flesh, dwells all manner of evil thoughts, wicked desires, and sinful wishes. This evil is with me constantly and tarnishes my best efforts to do Your will; it plagues my conscience with guilt and shame. I come to You this morning confessing my own weakness and asking You, for the sake of Your suffering and death, to forgive me, to overlook my shortcomings, and to help me in my daily struggle against the old sinful nature. Do not let my flesh direct my thoughts and actions. Lovingly strengthen me so that I can daily put off the old man and all that he works against me, and put on the new man born in Baptism and created after You in righteousness and holiness. Daily make me purer in my desires, cleaner in my speech, and holier in my actions, so that I may be blameless in Your sight and a shining light in the world until You call me home and to perfection. Amen. (12)

Thursday

EVENING

My help, O Lord, comes from You, who made both the heavens and the earth. You have been my refuge and strength during this day, a very present help in all trouble. You have given Your angels charge over me to keep me in all my ways. As night approaches, I know that You are my fortress, my God, in whom I trust. Though I lay down to rest, You neither slumber nor sleep. Let Your eyes be open and Your protecting hands be spread over my home and the homes of my neighbors. Give to the sick restful, refreshing sleep and to all who are sorrowful the consolation of Your gracious presence. Our time, our life, our salvation, O mighty and merciful God, are in Your hands. If the time allotted to me in this world is ended, if my last hour shall come this night, abide with me and preserve me in true faith. I know in whom I have believed: in You, my Father; and in my Lord Jesus Christ, who died for me; and in the Spirit, who preserves me. To You I commit my body and soul for safekeeping in time and in eternity; in Jesus' name. Amen. (13)

Friday

MORNING

Send me, O Lord, into the tasks of this day with a rejoicing heart. Teach me to labor diligently, to eat and drink to Your glory, and to think and plan to the ends You have laid out before me. That I may be truly fitted for the day, remind me again of the mighty work of my Savior, Jesus Christ, who redeemed me and in whom my sin is forgiven and my place with You forever assured. Impress upon my heart this day that while there is nothing holy about my life, my speech, or my faith without Your grace and mercy surrounding me, that with You I can faithfully help my neighbor and be of service to him. Teach me to look upon my life today as yet another opportunity to serve my fellowmen. Let me see in the routine of my daily tasks, in the need of my family and those who depend on me, in the want and struggle of the world about me, the good work You have prepared in advance for me to do. Grant that I be ready to forgive, earnest in rejoicing with those who are happy, quick in sympathy, and zealous in bearing the burdens of my fellowman; in Jesus' name. Amen. (14)

Friday

EVENING

Heavenly Father, I am Your child. Through Word and Sacrament I have been born anew. By Jesus' blood and sacrifice I have been received and adopted into Your family. Dear God, I admit I have not lived every moment of this day as becomes a child of Yours. There were times when I strayed, and self-will, negligence, lovelessness, and impurity found a resting place in my heart. I confess to You not only these sins but every sin with which I have offended You. O Father, I am not worthy to be called Your child. But I pray that You would, out of fatherly divine goodness and mercy, for the sake of Jesus' blood, forgive me my transgressions. Let my faith in this forgiveness be unwavering and sure. Let my gratitude to You be expressed in truth and in deed. Without Your peace I struggle under the burden of my sin and am lost, but with the joy of Your forgiveness I have all things. Comfort me in Your forgiving love, and preserve me steadfast in this faith now and forevermore. Amen. (15)

Saturday

MORNING

I lay down and slept; I woke again, for the Lord sustained me! Protected by Your mighty hand, I have passed the night. Lord, I am not worthy of the least of all the mercies You have shown me. As I thank You for all the gracious protection, I think of all those who are in sorrow and tribulation, in sickness, in poverty, in shame, in anguish of soul. I beseech You, the Father of our Lord Jesus Christ, the Father of mercies, and the God of all comfort, to comfort my brothers and sisters with the assurance of Your unchanging grace and loving-kindness. Strengthen their faith. Preserve them from misbelief, despair, and other great shame and vice. Teach them to humble themselves under Your mighty hand by recognizing Your gracious purpose to work through tribulation patience, through patience experience, through experience hope that will not make them ashamed. Help all sufferers to best their trials until at last Your kingdom comes. Deliver us all from every evil work and preserve us unto Your heavenly kingdom; in the name of Jesus. Amen. (16)

Saturday

EVENING

Another week of life has passed. As I look back, how swiftly have the hours gone by! Certainly You have numbered our days and hold them in Your hand. Therefore, Lord, keep me in mind of my life's end, the measure of my days, and what my life is, that I may know just how frail I am. We poor dying mortals come to You, eternal Lord, who has been our dwelling-place in all generations. From year to year You remain unchanged—the Lord God, merciful and gracious, long-suffering, and abundant in goodness and truth, keeping mercy for thousands, forgiving iniquity and transgression and sin. I come to You in this evening hour. I thank You that during the previous week Your compassion did not fail, that Your mercies were new every morning, and that You kept me in Your Word and grace. Shield me with Your mercy during the coming night so that I may again go to the house of God, receive Your Word and Sacrament, and with the voice of thanksgiving praise You and tell of all Your wondrous works; for Jesus' sake. Amen. (17)

Sunday

MORNING

Heavenly Father, who on this first of days called forth light out of darkness, shine into my soul with the power of Your love, give me a new heart, and create a clean spirit within me. Enlighten also my heart through Your Gospel to know You.

Glorious Savior, on this day You rose from death and the grave and proved Yourself the Redeemer of all the world; give me faith to trust You wholly for the forgiveness of all my sin, and grant me grace to rise to newness of life.

Holy Spirit, who on this day charged the Church with joyous faith and vigor, fill me also with Your healing, Your gift to speak, and Your strength to love.

O Holy Trinity, my glorious God, my strength and shield, set apart my heart to Your service this day, give to my worship sincerity and earnestness, and to my praise joy; grant that my fellow believers and I be kept at all times in the unity of faith, and refresh me with Your Word; in Jesus' name. Amen. (18)

Sunday

EVENING

Lord God, I thank You for the peace of this day, the peace proclaimed to me by Your Gospel, the peace from the strife and toil of daily tasks, the peace of coming to You in prayer. Dear God, let not this peace vanish from my heart and depart from my life. Let not the cares of this world nor its joys stifle the seedling of the Word that You have implanted in me. Let not the image of my Savior be defaced in me by doubt and sin, by waywardness, or by shame. Grant that the joy of worship may be steady and strong within me, even in the days when I may not be able to go to church with my fellow Christians. Grant that the sureness of Your peace may persist in my heart when the blasts of doubt and evil assail me. Give me refreshing rest this night, and fit me, body and soul, for the labors of this coming week; for Jesus' sake. Amen. (19)

Monday

MORNING

I thank You, heavenly Father, for the gift of rest and for the refreshment of body and soul that You have granted me in my worship of yesterday and my slumber of the night. I pray, make me ready to commit restored energies to the tasks that lie before me. Forgive me all my sins for Jesus' sake, and purge from my heart all selfish desires and purposes which would wrongly use my gifts and powers. Grant that I may, day by day, put forth efforts pleasing to You, helpful to my fellowmen, and sufficient to provide for my daily needs. Keep me mindful that my service to men is service to You. Help me to remember that in all things my sufficiency is of You and that whatever I do is to be done to Your glory. Give me joy in my labor, sincerity in my service, and unselfishness in all my striving. Help me to be faithful in all things; for the sake of Him who died for me. Amen. (20)

Monday

EVENING

Dear Savior, as I prepare for this night's rest, remind me again that You are with me. You have witnessed my life to this day, even the thoughts of my heart; O Savior, for the sake of Your precious blood blot out all my sins. Let them be accounted to Your charge and not to mine. Cleanse my conscience from all evil, and assure me of the fullness of my peace with God through You. Richly endow me with Your Spirit that I may not waver in my faith in You or doubt the reality of Your presence. Preserve me from idle worry, and keep me from faltering in my faith. Fill me with joy as I walk daily with You, seeing fulfilled the truth that You rule my world and life for my good. Protect and be with all for whom I care; defend my home, my community, and my country. Keep all people and me safe from violence and discord, war and crime. By Your Word stem the tide of sin and bring forgiveness and love into the world. Be my rest, my peace, and my all. Amen. (21)

Tuesday

MORNING

Again, O heavenly Father, You have granted me strength to rise to the tasks of the day. I thank You for Your mercy and love. Without Your power upholding me I should be unable to live. Give me a spirit of gratitude for all Your gifts. Above all, dear Father, keep me grateful for the gift of the forgiveness of all my sins through the merits of Jesus Christ, Your Son and my Savior. Grant that whatever need, whatever sorrow may beset my day, my faith in this forgiveness may remain steadfast and firm. Let no grief or pain, no doubt or gloom, come between me and the certainty of Your love. If it is Your purpose to try me this day with difficulties for the body or the heart, grant that I may, by Your Spirit, conquer in this trial and hold fast to Your mercy, knowing that the sufferings of this time are not worthy to be compared with the glory You have in store for me. Make Your Word my joy, Your counsel my guide, Your presence my peace; in Jesus Christ. Amen. (22)

Tuesday

EVENING

Dear Father in heaven, as I look this evening upon the hours of the day just past, I am aware of the many ways in which I have offended You in word and deed and of the many opportunities for service and love in which I have failed. Forgive me these trespasses and shortcomings for Jesus' sake. I am particularly mindful of the ways in which I have failed to testify of Your glorious name and to witness of Your love in Christ Jesus to men. Give me grace, heavenly Father, to overcome this lack of love, this slowness to confess You, this sluggishness in winning souls. Make Christians everywhere zealous to work while it is day in leading others into Your kingdom. Protect all in their Christian profession—all pastors and teachers, all missionaries and others who strive for the Gospel. Preserve peace among men that Your Gospel may run swiftly. If You would tonight make an end of my earthly journey, take me to You; and if I am to rise to Your service, fit me more fully. Hear me for the sake of Your Son, our divine Redeemer. Amen. (23)

Wednesday

MORNING

Lord God, You have given me another day, a day to live in Your service and for the good of my fellowmen, I am indeed a poor tool in Your hand and deserving to be cast aside. Forgive me all my sins for Jesus' sake, and by Your Spirit grant me the fitness to work for You this day. I beseech You to make me mindful, dear Lord, that I am but a stranger and a pilgrim in this present world. Let me not devote my efforts today to purposes unworthy of You; let me not gather treasures merely for this world; let me not serve mammon. This life is but a vain show; let me not search for an abiding city here. But, Lord, fasten my heart and hope on the life that is in You, and let my strivings and desires be directed to the treasures of Your love. As long as I am in the land of my pilgrimage, hold my hand, Lord; keep me from every straying path. If I should stumble in sinful weakness, grant me repentance and faith; for Jesus' sake. Amen. (24)

Wednesday

EVENING

Heavenly Father, as I come to the close of this day, I bow my head to receive Your benediction, eternal caretaker of my body and soul. Shut out all sins that would cling to me, and wash me in Christ's precious blood from all my iniquities. Remove the worries and the cares of the day, and fill my soul with contentment and peace. Enter in and take full possession of my heart, that, standing in Your grace, I may be faithful, trusting, and forgiving. Watch over me and over all Your own during this coming night, and preserve our homes from danger and destruction. Bless all Your children, and let Your divine presence give strength to the sick and consolation to the suffering. I ask this of You as my heavenly Father in the name of Jesus Christ, my Savior and Redeemer. Amen. (25)

Thursday

MORNING

The day has dawned, O Father in heaven, and everywhere Your children are lifting holy hands to You for strength for the day and cheer on the road. Let my prayers be acceptable to You for the sake of Jesus Christ, my Savior, through whose merits my peace has been made with You. Let the Daystar rise in my heart, O Lord, by faith in that Savior through whom my place with You is sure forevermore. I beseech You, let not only my prayer but also my whole life, my every act, thought, and word, be a sacrifice to You today, unblemished and worthy, through the power of Your Spirit. Let the message of Your Word fill me with the assurance of the forgiveness of my sin; let the counsel of Your revealed will point out to me the way I am to go; let Your Spirit give me courage and strength to choose the good part every hour. Hold me in oneness of faith with my fellow Christians, and let me be salt that has not lost its saltiness. Keep me Yours for the sake of Your Son, my Redeemer. Amen. (26)

Thursday

EVENING

Dear Savior, You have purchased me with Your blood that I may live in Your kingdom and be an heir of life eternal. You have seized me that I may ever more perfectly lay hold of the newness of life wherewith I am to serve You. Again I have been given a day in which to peruse the prize of this high calling. Where I have faltered on the road or grown weary in the search, O Lord, forgive me for the sake of Your infinite compassion. You know the weakness of my heart, O Christ, and will not reject my plea for mercy. Give me, according to Your good pleasure, rest from the rigors of my toil this day. Renew me also from the weariness of sin. Let Your Word nourish me, let the Water of life refresh my parched soul, and let me become more joyful, more complete, in the quest for holiness. Grant that my prayers come before You with more persistence and greater faith; make me ever mindful that my whole life is hidden in You with God. I trust in You; You will never forsake me. Amen. (27)

Friday

MORNING

Heavenly Father, in the name of Jesus, my Savior, I approach You in this morning hour, beseeching You to let Your grace and mercy go with me through the day. Let Your presence give me the blessed assurance of Your divine protection amid dangers, guidance amid uncertainty, and strength against temptations. Bless the labors of my hands. Bless our home with Your continued presence. Bless our nation, and let righteousness and peace prevail. Bless Your Church, and keep her in Your Word and truth. Bless our schools, and grant that boys and girls may grow in grace and knowledge of You and Your will. Remember not the sins of my youth nor my many trespasses. Bring me safely home tonight, and keep me steadfast in faith; through Jesus Christ, my Redeemer. Amen. (28)

Friday

EVENING

Almighty God, Father, Son, and Holy Spirit, as the light of the day fades away and the darkness comes, I know that You, who kept safe Israel, will neither slumber nor sleep. With my thanksgivings I exalt You as the source of the many blessings of this day. Teach me to see ever more clearly that life and happiness, health and daily bread, peace of heart, forgiveness of sins, and the promise of life forever with You are gifts of Your divine grace. Continue Your mercies toward me, my fellow believers, and all mankind. If I have enemies, bless them and let them undergo a change of heart. Pardon the sin of my transgressions and shortcomings for the sake of Jesus, my Redeemer. Strengthen Your Church, and let her membership constantly grow and praise You, the only true God, here in time and hereafter in eternity; in Jesus' name. Amen. (29)

Saturday

MORNING

I thank You, heavenly Father, for setting Your angel to guard my slumber during the night past and for the day of grace and service into which You have awakened me. Keep me steadfast in the awareness of Your protection and in faith in the redemptive work of Jesus Christ, Your Son. Lord, make me mindful of the temptations of sinful care, selfishness, and impure desires, which beset me on every side and from within. Help me in this hour to put on anew the armor of light, that I may be fitted with every weapon of offense and defense against the perils that threaten my spiritual life. Let Your Gospel call me with new sweetness to be reconciled to You; let Your Spirit call me with new power to follow You. Teach me to live this day as though it is my last on earth, knowing that whether I live or whether I die I am present with You. Be my Protector, my Guide, and my Father; for Jesus' sake. Amen. (30)

Saturday
EVENING

Heavenly Father, once more I would bring to You the load of a week's sins, and I pray, for the sake of the limitless merit of Christ Jesus, bury my guilt and punishment deep in His wounds. By Your mercy You have granted me rich opportunities to work in Your vineyard, but I have fallen short of that unselfish love that Your Law demands. I praise and thank You, heavenly Father, that my salvation rests altogether on Your grace and mercy and not on my efforts and achievements. I pray, let the message of the Gospel and the power of the Sacrament increase faithfulness to You. As it is Your will, grant me opportunity to worship You in Your sanctuary tomorrow, and graciously prepare my heart to receive Your Word with meekness and the Spirit's work with joy. Let not the vanity of this present world turn me from You and the means of grace that spring forth in rich supply from Your heavenly treasures. Father, I thank You for Your love; let my whole life serve You. Amen. (31)

Sunday

MORNING

Eternal, almighty God and Father, I give You heartfelt praise and thanks that You have graciously preserved me from all evil and danger to body and soul during the past night and all time previously by means of Your holy angels. I now earnestly beseech You to forgive me all my sins, with which I have ever offended You, and enlighten me by Your Holy Spirit, that I may daily grow in the knowledge of You. Bestow Your grace upon me, that I may be defended throughout this coming day from all sin and disgrace. May it be found in Your divine will that I also may walk in Your path, that being thus protected from all evil, I may always and unceasingly keep You in my heart and in my thoughts. When my hour of death draws near and I must depart this life, may You then let me joyfully fall asleep unto eternal life in the true knowledge of Your dear Son, Jesus Christ. Amen. (32)

Sunday

EVENING

Lord, almighty God and heavenly Father, I thank You from the bottom of my heart for all the fatherly gifts and kind favors that You have shown me today and that You have preserved me from all evil. As Your dear child, I ask that You would graciously keep me in Your Word, which alone brings salvation, until the sigh of my last breath. Illumine my heart with Your Holy Spirit, that I may discern the good and the evil. And may all my sins, those that I have knowingly committed and those that remain hidden to me, be forgotten in Your mercy. Give to me this coming night a peace that comes from knowing You, that I may awake again refreshed and healthy in order to praise You. Dear Father, grant me grace that my life may be pleasing to You and befitting the salvation won for me in Jesus Christ, Your dear Son, my one and only Lord. Amen. (33)

Monday

MORNING

O just and faithful God and heavenly Father, I praise and honor You from the depths of my heart that You have allowed me to rest and sleep safely this past night and that through Your fatherly love, You have awakened me again refreshed and healthy. It is my heartfelt prayer that You would graciously protect me, together with my dear family and all Christians, from all evil and danger to the body and to the soul, that everyday I may be found to be in Your will. I commend myself, my body and soul, heart, intellect, will and thoughts, all my efforts, my life and death, and everything that I am and have, into Your divine protection. May Your holy angels be and remain by me, that no misfortune of body or soul may assail me. This grant me for the sake of Jesus Christ, Your dear Son. Amen. (34)

Monday

EVENING

Merciful God, gracious Father, I thank You that You have graciously protected me today, even to this very hour, from all misfortune of body and soul. For the sake of Jesus Christ, Your dear Son, forgive me all my sins on account of grace, for this day I have repeatedly worked against You in thought, word, and deed, while failing to consider the eternal consequences. Grant that I may lie down to a safe rest and a peaceful sleep, preserved by Your fatherly care and Your almighty power from every assault against my body and soul. Defend me against the cunning and power of the devil; keep me free from bad, useless, and shameful dreams. As it be Your will, awaken me refreshed and healthy to praise You another day. Now, into Your divine hand I commend myself entirely. You have redeemed me, O faithful God. Amen. (35)

Tuesday

MORNING

O Lord Jesus Christ, only Savior of the world, to You I lift up my heart, will, and intellect, and I thank You again and again that, through Your boundless grace, You have protected me through the night against the cunning and power of the enemy and that I have awakened once again restored and fit. O Lord Jesus Christ, You who are my possession and inheritance, my salvation is in Your hands. I do not know of any other helper, whether in heaven or on earth, save You alone. Therefore, I implore You on account of Your unspeakable martyrdom, suffering, and most humiliatingly bitter death, that You would be gracious and merciful to me, both today and for the rest of my life. You, dearest Jesus Christ, have suffered out of great love for me, a poor sinner. Forgive all my transgressions against You. Protect me and keep me safe from sin and from every evil, until You graciously call me away to eternal joy and salvation; hear me on account of Your most holy name. Amen. (36)

Tuesday

EVENING

O eternal, merciful, and bounteous God of heaven, I thank You that out of surpassing grace and fatherly care You have allowed me to complete another day in fitness and soundness. I confess that this day I have not added to Your honor and praise, nor have I shown myself to be sufficiently useful to my neighbor, all because my corrupted nature favors evil instead of good. Therefore, forgive me, O faithful God, that I, born of sinful seed, may yet take part in Your grace. Teach me often to contemplate my own end that I thus may be found to be truly contrite. When that end does draw near, let me depart from this vale of tears as one comforted and blessed and find a place among all believing Christians in the heavenly paradise. Take me under Your almighty protection as long as I have days numbered upon the earth. Graciously defend and preserve me from all injury and danger to body and soul for the sake of Jesus Christ, Your dear Son. Amen. (37)

Wednesday

MORNING

O almighty, merciful God, gracious Father in heaven, You once again have defended me this night through the protection of Your holy angels, so that I have lived to see yet another day refreshed and sound. For that, I give You thanks and praise. Let all my doings and my will match Yours, and of Your great mercy, forgive me the miserable sin that accompanies me. Govern with Your Holy Spirit all my efforts, heart, intellect, desires, and thoughts, all my words and works, that I might understand that which is good and that which is evil. May I also be able to live and find my way today in this evil and perverted world, so that, above all else, forgiven of my sins, I may carry a heartfelt longing for the eternal heavenly home that has been purchased and won for me by Christ, my Savior. May I not belittle, fritter away, and finally lose that with my sinful life. To that end, graciously help me with Your divine love and the power of the Holy Spirit; for the sake of Your dear Son, Jesus Christ. Amen. (38)

Wednesday

EVENING

I thank You, O most mighty God, most benevolent Father, that again You have graciously protected me throughout the day against all injury and evil of body and soul. Out of Your divine goodness, cover my sin with Christ's atonement! Do not forsake me, Your creation, on account of everything that I have done with heart, mouth, or whatever else against You and Your holy commandments. Forgive me my wrongdoing and restore to me the hope of my salvation—salvation that You have dearly purchased by the blood of Your dearest Son, Jesus Christ. Shelter me this night under Your wings of grace, and protect me against the evil enemy who seeks after me like a roaring lion intent on devouring me. All this I pray that I may rest and sleep securely under the shadow of Your goodness and mercy and that the evil enemy may not be permitted to draw near to me and do me any kind of harm; through Jesus Christ, Your Son. Amen. (39)

Thursday

MORNING

God the Father, God the Son, and God the Holy Spirit, O Holy Trinity worthy of praise, to You I offer myself with body and soul from this moment on, even unto eternity. I give You praise and thanks that You have not permitted the enemy to come and harm me in the night, but rather, through the protection of Your dear angels, I have been preserved. With what could I possibly repay You? How might I praise You for this? I will give You a shattered heart full of fear, a heart full of blood-red sins, with penitence and contrition. I do so, that You may graciously receive it and wash it white as snow with the noble blood of Your dear Son, my Redeemer. I do so, that You might hide it away in His holy, sinless wounds and thus return to me the gracious forgiveness of all my sins. Help me today and every day that I may remain in Christian readiness, for I cannot know when and how You shall come and call me away from this life, so that I may be led to eternal joy. Such things grant to me, O gracious God and Father, on account of Your dear Son, Jesus Christ. Amen. (40)

Thursday

EVENING

Merciful, tenderhearted God, eternal Father, You bear such a heartfelt love and fatherly care for me, a poor sinner, that You graciously defended me in every day and hour from my youth until the present against all manner of the devil's cunning and danger and injury from a godless, evil world. I ask You in all humility and according to Your fatherly love, that You would not think anymore on all the things that I have done against You. I ask rather that You grant me a jubilee remission on account of Your grace. Be gracious to me for the sake of Your dear Son, Jesus Christ, who became the deposit against all my sins. This night, guard me and all for whom I care against an evil, sudden death, against emergency by fire or flood, against pestilence and all other calamity. I commend myself, my body and soul and everything I have into Your fatherly protection. May Your holy angels be with me, that I fear no ill fortune. Amen. (41)

Friday

MORNING

In Your name, O crucified Lord Jesus Christ, I now arise from sleep. You suffered the all-painful death on the trunk of the holy cross as the true, patient, sacrificial Lamb for me. You have bought my freedom from all my sins, death, the devil, and hell through Your rose-colored blood. Rule my heart by Your Holy Spirit, refreshing it with the heavenly dew of Your grace. Preserve me with Your divine love and hide me—body and soul—in Your holy wounds. Wash me clean of all my sins, maintain me in every good work, and lead me out of the vale of tears that is this world into eternal joy and glory, O faithful Savior, Jesus Christ, my only solace, hope, and life. Amen. (42)

Friday

EVENING

O Lord Jesus Christ, patient sacrificial Lamb, You are the holy atonement-offering for all my sins, yet not just for mine alone, but also for the sins of the whole world! I thank You once again that You have kept me in body and soul under Your divine protection this day. I beseech You graciously to pardon and forgive all the sins I have committed this day out of the weakness of my corrupted nature and from the encouragement of the evil one. They are a heavy burden and press upon my heart and conscience. As I prepare to lie down to rest and sleep, stretch out Your wings of grace over me. Help me, that I might sleep under them in peace and rest according to the body, yet according to the soul be ever awake and inclined to You, being ever mindful of Your majestic future advent at the final judgment. Strengthen me to wait upon You with heartfelt sighs until that time when I shall blessedly depart from here to be with You.

To that end, help me, O faithful Savior, You who, with the Father and Holy Spirit, are most highly praised unto all eternity. Amen. (43)

Saturday

MORNING

Faithful Father in heaven, I have neither the power nor the ability to praise and thank You enough for all the loving-kindness that You have so graciously shown me my entire life. I am but flesh and blood that can do nothing but evil. Yet You allow an abundant flow of gifts to come to me every day, especially in the past night when You were my shield and my support. Were that not so, the power of the devil surely would have struck me so severe a blow that I could not have hoped to arise again in sound condition. Yet through Your gracious protection I have been defended in a manner unsurpassed. I beseech You from the utmost depths of my being that You would let Your grace flow over me and defend me. I am Yours by the blood of Christ, from now unto eternal life. Amen. Amen. Lord Jesus, take my soul into Your hands and let me be commended unto You. Amen. (44)

Saturday

EVENING

Merciful, gracious God and Father, once again I give You praise and thanks that You have, out of fatherly love, guarded me my entire life and have graciously protected me throughout this day and this entire week from all misfortune of body and soul. I ask You that, by Your grace offered to all penitent sinners, You would cover all my sins that I have committed against You and my neighbor today and this past week, both those known and those unknown. Think upon them nevermore. Help me graciously to enter into a new Christian life that would please You and all the holy angels in heaven as I leave this week behind. Let me be commended to Your gracious arms in the coming night, that I may take my rest and sleep in safety, to wake again fresh and sound to praise You. And when the hour of my death is upon me, take me to You, through my Lord Jesus Christ, for I am Yours and You are mine; how I long heartily to be near You soon! Amen. (45)

Sunday

MORNING

Our Father who art in heaven, hallowed be Thy name. Yes, Lord God, dear Father, hallowed be Your name, both in us and throughout the whole world. Destroy and root out the abominations, idolatry, and heresy of those who war against the Church: all false teachers and the divisive spirits who wrongly use Your name and in shameful ways take it in vain. They horribly blaspheme and insistently boast that in Your name they teach Your Word, when in reality it is the devil's deceit and trickery in the guise of Your name by which they seduce many poor souls throughout the world, even killing and shedding much innocent blood, and in such persecution they believe that they render You a divine service.

Dear Lord God, convert and restrain them, that together we may hallow and praise Your name both with true and pure doctrine and with a good and holy life. Restrain those who are unwilling to be converted so that they are forced to cease from misusing, defiling, and dishonoring Your holy name and from misleading the poor people. Amen. (46)

Sunday
EVENING

Lord God, heavenly Father, there is nothing hidden from You. Even my secret thoughts You know from a distance. With You the darkness of night is like daylight. In the consciousness of my many sins and of Your all searching eye, I therefore come to You again this night, confessing my many shortcomings and faults. How far my mind wandered away from the green pastures of Your sacred Word this holy day! How feeble have been my meditations on the things that belong to my temporal and my everlasting peace! All this and more You know better than I can tell it. But You are gracious ever to forgive my sin. O Lord, I take refuge in Your fatherly goodness in Jesus' name. For His sake forgive and help me. Amen. (47)

Forgive me, Lord, for Thy dear Son,
The ill that I this day have done;
That with the world, myself, and Thee,
I, ere I sleep, at peace may be.
(LSB 883:2)

Monday

MORNING

Our Father who art in heaven, Thy kingdom come. O dear Lord, God and Father, You see how the wisdom and reason of the world not only profane Your name but also take the power, might, and wealth You have given for ruling the world and serving You and use them in opposition to Your kingdom. They trouble and hinder the tiny flock of Your kingdom that is weak, despised, and few in number. They will not tolerate Your flock on earth.

Dear Lord, God and Father, convert and restrain them. Convert those who are still to become children and members of Your kingdom, so that together we may serve You in Your kingdom in true faith and true love and that from our life here we may enter into Your eternal kingdom. Restrain those who will not turn away their might and power from the destruction of Your kingdom, so when they are cast down from their seats of power and are being humbled, they will cease their efforts. Amen. (48)

Monday

EVENING

Lord, let my prayers be set before You as incense and the lifting up of my hands as the evening sacrifice. Throughout this coming night, give me Your great peace. Preserve me from all terror and from all evil that walks in the darkness. Deliver my heart from all evil imaginations. Grant unto me sweet sleep to rest and refresh me. In the morning awaken me, Lord, with renewed strength and bless me with Your Spirit to walk again in the ways of Your commandments. And may Your blessings attend my ways! Amen. (49)

I need Thy presence ev'ry passing hour;
What but Thy grace can foil the tempter's pow'r?
Who like Thyself my guide and stay can be?
Through cloud and sunshine, O, abide with me.
(LSB 878:2)

Tuesday

MORNING

Our Father who art in heaven, Thy will be done on earth as it is in heaven. O dear Lord, You know that if the world cannot destroy Your name or Your kingdom, there are those who work day and night with tricks, fraud, and many strange conspiracies to try and do so. They encourage and support every evil intention raging against Your name, Your Word, Your kingdom, and Your children, threatening to destroy them.

Therefore, dear Lord, God and Father, convert and restrain them. Convert those who have yet to acknowledge Your good will, that together with them we may obey Your will. Let us gladly and patiently bear every cross and adversity and thereby acknowledge, test, and experience Your good, gracious, and perfect will. Constrain those who seek to harm us, and turn against them their own tricks and devices, as we sing:

> *He makes a pit, digging it out, and falls into the hole that he has made. His mischief returns upon his own head, and on his own skull his violence descends. I will give to the* LORD *the thanks due to His righteousness, and I will sing praise to the name of the* LORD, *the Most High*
> (PSALM 7:15–17). *Amen.* (50)

Tuesday

EVENING

Lord God, heavenly Father, by Your grace I was born again of water and the Spirit. I pray this night that You would forgive the many sins that I have committed, often forgetting the promises You made to me in my Baptism. Strengthen me again by Your Holy Spirit, the Spirit of power and strength, so that in daily contrition and repentance I may walk and live before You in righteousness and in purity. Hold me again this night against every enemy, both seen and unseen. Speak against the night's surging seas that may threaten my life and say to them and to me, "Peace, be still." Hear me, my Lord and God. Amen. (51)

Teach me to live that I may dread
The grave as little as my bed.
Teach me to die that so I may
Rise glorious at the awe-full day.
(*LSB* 883:3)

Wednesday

MORNING

Our Father who art in heaven, give us this day our daily bread. Dear Lord, God and Father, grant us Your blessing in our temporal and physical life. Graciously grant us blessed peace. Protect us against war and disorder. Grant to our president success against our enemies. Grant him wisdom and understanding to administer his duties and office in peace and happiness. Grant to all elected and appointed leaders good counsel and the will and ability to preserve this land and this people in tranquility and justice. Especially aid and guide the governor of this state, under whose protection You have sheltered us, so being protected against all harm, the administration may be blessed and we can live free from evil and disloyal people. Grant grace to all the people to serve our leaders loyally and obediently. Grant to all of us diligence in our vocation and charity in our dealings with one another. Grant us favorable weather and good harvest. I commend to You my house and home, spouse and children. Help me to manage my household well and support and educate my children as a Christian should. Defend us from the destroyer and his wicked angels, who work against us, looking for every opportunity to harm us and cause mischief in this life. Amen. (52)

Wednesday

EVENING

Dear Lord, abide with me, for it is toward evening, and the day is quickly ending. Grant unto me the blessedness that welcomes You and recognizes You in the breaking of bread and in the Holy Supper, which You have ordained for us to eat and to drink. Abide with me this night. Bread of life, feed my soul; Water of life, refresh me. Make me true to You, and in that peace grant that I may lie down and sleep. Lord, so abide with me. Amen. (53)

I fear no foe with Thee at hand to bless;
Ills have no weight, and tears no bitterness.
Where is death's sting? Where, grave, thy victory?
I triumph still if Thou abide with me!
(LSB 878:5)

Thursday

MORNING

Our Father who art in heaven, forgive us our trespasses, as we forgive those who trespass against us. O dear Lord, God and Father, do not enter into judgment against us, for in Your sight no one who lives is justified before You. Do not count it against us as sin that we are so unthankful for all Your indescribable spiritual and physical blessings. Do not judge us on account of our daily sin. We stumble and sin many more times than we even know or recognize. "For He who avenges blood is mindful of them; He does not forget the cry of the afflicted" (Psalm 9:12).

Look away from our accomplishments as well as our wickedness; in Your boundless compassion look instead upon Your dear Son, Jesus Christ. Forgive also those who are our enemies or who have wronged us, just as we forgive them from our hearts. By their actions against us, they arouse Your anger and hurt themselves, yet we are not helped by their ruin and would much rather that they be saved with us. Amen. (54)

Thursday

EVENING

Heavenly Father, the heavens declare Your glory, and the creation shows Your handiwork; day after day they speak of You, night after night they display Your wonders. There is nowhere we can go where they are not heard. Your Word is sweeter than these. Your words speak forgiveness; they promise eternal life and salvation. Though in weakness I sin again and again, You are ever faithful to Your Word and forgive my sin. Grant that I may find comfort again this night in Your faithfulness. Draw near to all penitent sinners and speak comfortingly to them this night. Be also with all my dear ones here and everywhere, and bless them. Amen. (55)

When in the night I sleepless lie,
My soul with heav'nly thoughts supply;
Let no ill dreams disturb my rest,
No pow'rs of darkness me molest.
(*LSB* 883:5)

Friday

MORNING

Our Father who art in heaven, lead us not into temptation. O dear Lord, Father and God, keep us prepared and alert, eager and diligent in Your Word and service, so that we do not become complacent and careless as though we had already achieved everything. We implore You by Your mercy not to let the devil sneak in and take away from us Your precious Word or stir up strife and factions among us, or otherwise lead us into spiritual and physical sin and disgrace. Grant us wisdom and strength through Your Spirit that we may bravely resist the devil and gain the victory. Amen. (56)

Friday

EVENING

Blessed Savior, You spilled Your blood to redeem me from death. Having been lifted up on the cross, You draw all men to Yourself. You have drawn me to Yourself by Your grace through Baptism. How could I refrain from loving You who so loved me that You did die for me! Gracious Savior, continue to draw me to You. Draw me out of every night of sin into the daylight of Your truth and love. Draw me out of the power of the evil one, out of evil passions and desires, and out of the many cares of this world and life in it. Draw me to the Holy Feast, where You give to me Your body and blood for the forgiveness of my sin; draw me daily into the grace of my Baptism. Yes, Lord, draw me unto You. Amen. (57)

Swift to its close ebbs out life's little day;
Earth's joys grow dim, its glories pass away;
Change and decay in all around I see;
O Thou who changest not, abide with me.
(*LSB* 878:4)

Saturday

MORNING

Our Father who art in heaven, deliver us from evil. O dear Lord, God and Father, Your Son defeated sin, death, and the devil so that I may enjoy the fruits of His labor. You are faithful to me as You keep me in Your grace. Grant me faithfulness in this life, especially when I experience the attacks of the devil through misery and misfortune, uncertainty and evil. Should I grow weary of life and long for death, give me strength and confidence in my dear Savior's victory over sin, death, and the devil. And, when my last hour comes, mercifully grant me a blessed departure from this valley of sorrow. Grant that in the face of death I do not loose heart or fear it, but, with certain trust and hope in You, remain confident that You will take my soul into Your hands; for the sake of my Savior, Jesus Christ. Amen. (58)

Saturday

EVENING

Lord Jesus, blessed Advocate with the Father, who sits at His right hand to make intercession for us against sin, speak into my soul, through Your Holy Spirit in Your Word, the sweet consolations of Your all-sufficient atonement for my sins. Let me hear again Your convincing love: "Your sins are forgiven!" In such confidence let me go to sleep in peace and quietness. And in the morning wake me to the spiritual refreshment of another Sunday, with rest for both soul and body. Hear me, Lord Jesus, who together with the Father and the Holy Spirit are one Lord, to whom be glory forever! Amen. (59)

Hold thou Thy cross before my closing eyes,
Shine through the gloom, and point me to the skies;
Heav'n's morning breaks, and earth's vain shadows flee;
In life, in death, O Lord, abide with me.
(*LSB* 878:6)

OUR LIFE *of* WORSHIP

Remembrance of Baptism

THE APOSTLES' CREED

I believe in God, the Father Almighty, maker of heaven and earth.

And in Jesus Christ, His only Son, our Lord, who was conceived by the Holy Spirit, born of the Virgin Mary, suffered under Pontius Pilate, was crucified, died and was buried. He descended into hell. The third day He rose again from the dead. He ascended into heaven and sits at the right hand of God the Father Almighty. From thence He will come to judge the living and the dead.

I believe in the Holy Spirit, the holy Christian Church, the communion of saints, the forgiveness of sins, the resurrection of the body, and the life everlasting. Amen.

LUTHER'S EXPLANATION OF THE THREE ARTICLES OF THE CREED*

I believe that God has made me and all creatures; that He has given me my body and soul, eyes, ears, and all my members, my reason and all my senses, and still takes care of them. He also gives me clothing and shoes, food and drink, house and home, wife and children, land, animals, and all I have. He richly and daily provides me with all that I need to support this body and life. He defends me against all danger and guards and protects me from all evil. All this He does only out of fatherly, divine goodness and mercy, without any merit or worthiness in me. For all this it is my duty to thank and praise, serve and obey Him. This is most certainly true.

I believe that Jesus Christ, true God, begotten of the Father from eternity, and also true man, born of the Virgin Mary, is my Lord, who has redeemed me, a lost and condemned person, purchased and won me from all sins, from death, and from the power of the devil; not with gold or silver, but with His holy, precious blood and with His innocent suffering and death, that I may be His own and live under Him in His kingdom and serve Him in everlasting righteousness, innocence, and blessedness, just as He is risen from the dead, lives and reigns to all eternity. This is most certainly true.

I believe that I cannot by my own reason or strength believe in Jesus Christ, my Lord, or come to Him; but the Holy Spirit has called me by the Gospel, enlightened me with His gifts, sanctified and kept me in the true faith. In the same way He calls, gathers, enlightens, and sanctifies the whole Christian Church on earth, and keeps it with Jesus Christ in the one true faith. In this Christian Church He daily and richly forgives all my sins and the sins of all believers. On the Last Day He will raise me and all the dead, and give eternal life to me and all believers in Christ. This is most certainly true.

*From Luther's Small Catechism.

LUTHER'S EXPLANATION OF BAPTISM*

I. THE NATURE OF BAPTISM

What is Baptism?

Baptism is not just plain water, but it is the water included in God's command and combined with God's word.

Which is that word of God?

Christ our Lord says in the last chapter of Matthew: "Therefore go and make disciples of all nations, baptizing them in the name of the Father and of the Son and of the Holy Spirit." (Matthew 28:19)

II. THE BLESSINGS OF BAPTISM

What benefits does Baptism give?

It works forgiveness of sins, rescues from death and the devil, and gives eternal salvation to all who believe this, as the words and promises of God declare.

Which are these words and promises of God?

Christ our Lord says in the last chapter of Mark: "Whoever believes and is baptized will be saved, but whoever does not believe will be condemned." (Mark 16:16)

III. THE POWER OF BAPTISM

How can water do such great things?

Certainly not just water, but the word of God in and with the water does these things, along with the faith which trusts this word of God in the water. For without God's word the water is plain water and no Baptism. But with the word of God it is a Baptism, that is, a life-giving water, rich in grace, and a washing of the new birth in the Holy Spirit, as St. Paul says in Titus chapter three: "He saved us through the washing of rebirth and renewal by the Holy Spirit, whom He poured out on us generously through Jesus Christ our Savior, so that, having been justified by His grace, we might become heirs having the hope of eternal life. This is a trustworthy saying." (Titus 3:5–8)

IV. THE SIGNIFICANCE OF BAPTIZING WITH WATER

What does such baptizing with water indicate?

It indicates that the Old Adam in us should by daily contrition and repentance be drowned and die with all sins and evil desires, and that a new man should daily emerge and arise to live before God in righteousness and purity forever.

Where is this written?

St. Paul writes in Romans chapter six: "We were therefore buried with Him through baptism into death in order that, just as Christ was raised from the dead through the glory of the Father, we too may live a new life." (Romans 6:4)

*From Luther's Small Catechism.

MEDITATION ON LUTHER'S EXPLANATION OF HOLY BAPTISM

Father, Son, and Holy Spirit, in whose name we have been baptized and made disciples: we thank You for our Baptism, which we know is not ordinary water but the water comprehended in Your command and connected with Your Word. How precious are the gifts and benefits it confers. It works forgiveness of sins, delivers from death and the devil, and confers everlasting salvation on all who believe as Your Word and promises declare. Have You not said, Lord Jesus: "Whoever believes and is baptized will be saved, but whoever does not believe will be condemned" (Mark 16:16)? Let us, having been baptized, believe, that we may be saved.

Oh, wondrous are the effects of this simple act—effects produced not by water, but by the Word of God connected with the water. Without the Word of God, the water is simply water and no Baptism. But when connected with the Word of God, it is Baptism, that is, a gracious water of life and a washing of regeneration in the Holy Spirit, as St. Paul said to Titus: "He saved us . . . according to His own mercy, by the washing of regeneration and renewal of the Holy Spirit, whom He poured out on us richly through Jesus Christ our Savior, so that being justified by His grace we might become heirs according to the hope of eternal life. The saying is trustworthy" (Titus 3:5–8).

O God, who has taught us by Your holy apostle that we were buried with Christ by Baptism into death, that just as He was bodily raised up from the dead by the glory of the Father, so we also should walk in newness of life: grant that we may walk in the grace of our Baptism, so that the old Adam in us may be drowned and destroyed by daily sorrow and repentance, together with all sins and evil lusts, and that again a new man may daily come forth and rise, who shall live in the presence of God in righteousness and purity forever; through Jesus Christ, Your well-beloved Son, our Savior, who lives and reigns with You and the Holy Spirit, one God, world without end. Amen. (60)

PRAYER IN REMEMBRANCE OF HOLY BAPTISM

Dear Father in heaven, You have adopted me as Your very own and given me Your name in the waters of my Holy Baptism. You have generously poured out upon me Your Holy Spirit through Your Son, my only Savior, Jesus Christ. By the washing of the water with Your Word, I have been united with Him in His death. Just as surely do I have a share in His resurrection and His never-ending life. For His sake You have called me a beloved child and declared me to be well-pleasing in Your sight. For all of this I thank and praise You.

Yet, my old Adam remains, with all my sinful desires, while the devil and the world seek to entice me away from You. Only You can help me and save me. Be gracious to me; guard and protect me from all evil. Surround me with Your holy angels; keep the devil at bay, and all his works and all his ways far from me.

Return me always to the saving waters of my Holy Baptism, and thereby drown and destroy the old Adam within me. By Your Word and Holy Spirit, bring me daily to contrition and repentance, and by Your free and full forgiveness of my sins, strengthen and sustain my faith and lift me up with Your dear Son to that new life that shows forth Your praise; through the same Jesus Christ, my Lord. Amen. (61)

PARENT'S PRAYER ON CONFIRMATION

Almighty Father, You have given Your Church the gift of salvation through Baptism and faith. You have given this child of ours new birth by water and the Spirit, and You have made him (her) Your own child. By Your grace and in Your Church, You have nurtured him (her) in the faith through Your Gospel and Sacraments. I thank You for all Your goodness and faithfulness in leading him (her) to this day. I rejoice that today he (she) professes the one, true faith in the company of You and Your Church. I fervently pray that he (she) will always profess this faith, be sustained in the faith by Your means of grace, and rejoice that he (she) is Your beloved child, a child redeemed by Your beloved Son and sanctified by Your Holy Spirit, so that he (she) may inherit eternal salvation and forever sing Your praises. Amen. (62)

CONFIRMAND'S PRAYER

Lord God, heavenly Father, You called me by name and declared that I was Your child through the washing of my Baptism. I desire to receive the true body and blood of my Savior, Jesus Christ, in the Sacrament of the Altar. Grant me grace that I may stand before the Church and faithfully speak of the hope that is mine through the life, death, and resurrection of Your Son. Strengthen me through Your Holy Spirit, that I can stand before Your altar and make my vow of fidelity, confident that through faith in You I receive the forgiveness of sins and the ability to do that which pleases You and brings honor and praise to Your name; through Jesus Christ, my Lord. Amen. (63)

PRAYER IN REMEMBRANCE OF CONFIRMATION

O Lord God and Father in heaven, I rejoice that through the waters of Baptism You made me Your own child and by Your grace You have brought me to faith in Christ Jesus. As I remember the day of my confirmation, I rejoice in Your gifts: You have made me Your own, You made me a member of the body of Christ, and by Your grace You have sustained me in the faith with Your Gospel and Sacraments. It is by Your grace that I am able to profess this faith. I pray that You will keep me faithful to my vows to the Church and help me to stand strong in the faith. Help me to receive Your gifts of forgiveness, life, and salvation with humility and gratitude. Help me to always rely on the words of Your beloved Son and on His body and blood to sustain me in the faith. Grant all this, so that I may stand before Your throne on the Last Day, redeemed and sanctified, ready to forever feast at the marriage banquet of the Lamb. Amen. (64)

Preparation for Confession and Absolution

THE TEN COMMANDMENTS*

THE FIRST COMMANDMENT

You shall have no other gods.

THE SECOND COMMANDMENT

You shall not misuse the name of the LORD your God.

THE THIRD COMMANDMENT

Remember the Sabbath day by keeping it holy.

THE FOURTH COMMANDMENT

Honor your father and your mother.

THE FIFTH COMMANDMENT

You shall not murder.

THE SIXTH COMMANDMENT

You shall not commit adultery.

THE SEVENTH COMMANDMENT

You shall not steal.

THE EIGHTH COMMANDMENT

You shall not give false testimony against your neighbor.

THE NINTH COMMANDMENT

You shall not covet your neighbor's house.

THE TENTH COMMANDMENT

You shall not covet your neighbor's wife, or his manservant or maidservant, his ox or donkey, or anything that belongs to your neighbor.

THE CLOSE OF THE COMMANDMENTS

What does God say about all these commandments? He says: "I, the LORD your God, am a jealous God, punishing the children for the sin of the fathers to the third and fourth generation of those who hate Me, but showing love to a thousand generations of those who love Me and keep My commandments." (Exodus 20:5–6)

*Quoted in Luther's Small Catechism. The text of the commandments is from Exodus 20:3, 7, 8, 12–17.

LUTHER'S EXPLANATION OF CONFESSION AND THE OFFICE OF THE KEYS*

What is Confession?

Confession has two parts. First, that we confess our sins, and second, that we receive absolution, that is, forgiveness, from the pastor as from God Himself, not doubting, but firmly believing that by it our sins are forgiven before God in heaven.

What sins should we confess?

Before God we should plead guilty of all sins, even those we are not aware of, as we do in the Lord's Prayer; but before the pastor we should confess only those sins which we know and feel in our hearts.

Which are these?

Consider your place in life according to the Ten Commandments: Are you a father, mother, son, daughter, husband, wife, or worker? Have you been disobedient, unfaithful, or lazy? Have you been hot-tempered, rude, or quarrelsome? Have you hurt someone by your words or deeds? Have you stolen, been negligent, wasted anything, or done any harm?

What is the Office of the Keys?

The Office of the Keys is that special authority which Christ has given to His Church on earth to forgive the sins of repentant sinners, but to withhold forgiveness from the unrepentant as long as they do not repent.

Where is this written?

This is what St. John the Evangelist writes in chapter twenty: The Lord Jesus breathed on His disciples and said, "Receive the Holy Spirit. If you forgive anyone his sins, they are forgiven; if you do not forgive them, they are not forgiven." (John 20:22–23)

What do you believe according to these words?

I believe that when the called ministers of Christ deal with us by His divine command, in particular when they exclude openly unrepentant sinners from the Christian congregation and absolve those who repent of their sins and want to do better, this is just as valid and certain, even in heaven, as if Christ our dear Lord dealt with us Himself.

*From Luther's Small Catechism.

BRIEF INSTRUCTION ON CONFESSION AND ABSOLUTION

My dear Christian, when you go to confession, do not be content with repeating a memorized confessional prayer or with having your pastor repeat it to you. Rather, bring along a penitent heart, from which your confession will flow. To offer confession when the heart is impenitent is mocking God. Without a penitent heart there is no forgiveness of sin.

The first requirement for a penitent heart is that you recognize your sins, feel sorry and repentant of them. By nature no man knows his sins, nor can he by his own doing cause repentance to spring from his heart. On the contrary, repentance comes from God. By nature we are far too blind, too indifferent, too careless, too self-righteous, too much absorbed in self-love and self-conceit, to plead guilty of all sins in the sight of God.

Above all things, therefore, bow your knees before God and call upon Him to open your eyes that you may thoroughly recognize the multitude and magnitude of your sins. Pray in the words of the sainted David: "Search me, O God, and know my heart! Try me and know my thoughts! And see if there be any grievous way in me, and lead me in the way everlasting!" (Psalm 139:23–24). Make a careful examination of your whole life according to the Ten Commandments. You will then soon find that you are a sinner. For even as a man does not see a spot on his face without a mirror, so he does not recognize his sins unless he sees himself in the mirror of the holy Ten Commandments. For every thought, every word, every deed against God's commandments is a sin, whether it consists in doing what God has forbidden or in failing to do what He has commanded.

But you must look not only at the large, external sins, but also those internal, secret digressions from God's commandments, the evil thoughts and desires of your heart. When examining yourself, being instant in prayer, you will discover that you did not fear, love, and trust in God as He demands; that you have not called upon God in prayer, praise, and thanksgiving so heartily and confidently as you should have done; that you have not properly heard and learned His Word and kept it sacred. You will find that you have not duly honored and obeyed your parents and superiors, but that you have been disobedient and discourteous toward them; that you have sinned against your neighbor by being angry, revengeful, and unforgiving; by entertaining unholy thoughts and desires; by showing envy, covetousness, and a sinful mind or by speaking slanderous words.

To sum up, you will come to know that you did not love your neighbor uprightly and heartily as yourself; rather, that self-love, quest for personal gain and honor, was the moving force of all your actions. Because of these and other sins you indeed have deserved God's wrath, His temporal and eternal punishment, if He would deal with you strictly according to justice. From these sins that you notice in yourself, you can infer how unclean and polluted your heart must be from which these sins flow; for the stream is no purer than its fountain, and by its fruits the tree is known. In this way you will come to a true knowledge of original sin.

Consider also the sins you do not know, but still have committed. They are far more numerous than those you do know. The omniscient God places all your sins in the light of His countenance. Knowing this, you certainly will be terrified in your conscience and experience sorrow and contrition for having offended your loving God so grievously and for having repaid His mercies with such dishonorable ingratitude.

The second part of repentance is faith, faith in Jesus Christ. It is He who has rendered full satisfaction for all your sins, procuring forgiveness of them all. Faith is, so to speak, the hand that appropriates forgiveness of sin and accepts it as an unmerited gift of divine grace. Without this faith all knowledge of sin and penitence over it are nothing but the repentance of a Cain and of a Judas and must end in despair. But by faith in Jesus Christ, the Savior of all sinners, the heart is comforted and satisfied. This faith, however, you cannot bring forth yourself; it is the work and gift of God the Holy Spirit. But if you feel that your faith is weak—you desire to believe, but you think you cannot—then pray to God to strengthen this faith of yours, which is battling against doubt. He is willing to do so and surely will give you a stronger faith, so that you will overcome all the doubts that are troubling your soul.

If you come to confession with such a penitent and believing heart, you will rejoice in the absolution spoken by your pastor. For your sins are really and truly forgiven by God in heaven. Such forgiveness of sins Christ has procured for all sinners by the shedding of His blood and by His death, and by His resurrection He sealed it to them. This He commanded to be preached throughout the world by means of the Gospel. Therefore when your pastor absolves you, he does nothing else than proclaim to you the Gospel of the forgiveness of sins. This, however, is not an empty announcement, but one actually offering and conveying the forgiveness of sins to the penitent sinner. Whenever, therefore, you hear your pastor pronounce absolution, do not doubt, but firmly believe, that your sins are forgiven before God in heaven. Believe it as firmly as though Christ were calling to you directly from heaven: "Take heart, My son [My daughter]; your sins are forgiven" (Matthew 9:2). For He says: "The one who hears you hears Me" (Luke 10:16); and: "If you forgive the sins of anyone, they are forgiven" (John 21:23).

Then the fruits of repentance are to follow. These consist in no longer knowingly and intentionally committing such sins as were forgiven you, but rather hating them, abstaining from them, and battling against them with the assistance of the Holy Spirit.

PRAYER BEFORE CONFESSION AND ABSOLUTION

Lord Jesus Christ, Son of God, have mercy on me, a sinner! Your Word is a lamp unto my feet and a light upon my path. It has laid bare my sin, for which I deserve nothing but punishment; yet, it has also declared to me Your grace and mercy and forgiveness.

As You have taught my heart to believe and trust in You, so shall I also confess with my mouth. Grant me the honesty to examine my life according to Your holy Ten Commandments, especially as they address my vocations in life. Discipline me as Your beloved child. Enable me to recognize my sin, to know and feel it in my heart, and rightly to bemoan and lament my iniquity and offenses. Give me both humility and courage to confess my sins and to receive from my pastor Your Holy Absolution, according to Your good and gracious will. Invigorate my faith, through this same word of forgiveness, to have no doubt, but firmly to believe, that by it all my sins are forgiven before God in heaven.

You have called and sent my pastor, in Your name and stead, to hear my confession with Your ears of mercy, and to forgive me with Your own voice. Since You have chosen to deal with me in this way, allow me not to neglect Your gift but to lay hold of it with eager confidence. Create in me a clean heart, O God, and restore to me the joy of Your salvation; for Your name's sake. Amen. (65)

AN ACT OF CONFESSION

O God, heavenly Father, I confess to You that I have grievously sinned against You in many ways, not only by my actions, but also by my thoughts and desires, which I cannot fully understand, but which are all known to You. I earnestly repent and am heartily sorry for all my many offenses against You. I pray, be gracious to me a poor miserable sinner! Out of Your goodness have mercy on me, and for the sake of Your dear Son, Jesus Christ, my Lord, forgive my sins, and strengthen me in love toward You and in service to my neighbor, that all I do may be pleasing in Your sight and bring praise to Your name; in Jesus' name I pray. Amen. (66)

Preparation for Worship

THE LORD'S PRAYER

Our Father who art in heaven, hallowed be Thy name, Thy kingdom come, Thy will be done on earth as it is in heaven. Give us this day our daily bread; and forgive us our trespasses as we forgive those who trespass against us; and lead us not into temptation, but deliver us from evil. For Thine is the kingdom and the power and the glory forever and ever. Amen. (67)

TE DEUM LAUDAMUS

We praise You, O God; we acknowledge You to be the Lord. All the earth now worships You, the Father everlasting. To You all angels cry aloud, the heavens and all the pow'rs therein. To You cherubim and seraphim continually do cry: Holy, holy, holy, Lord God of Sabaoth; heaven and earth are full of the majesty of Your glory. The glorious company of the apostles praise You. The goodly fellowship of the prophets praise You. The noble army of martyrs praise You. The holy Church throughout all the world does acknowledge You: The Father of an infinite majesty; Your adorable true and only Son; also the Holy Ghost, the Comforter. You are the king of glory, O Christ; You are the everlasting Son of the Father.

When You took upon Yourself to deliver man, You humbled Yourself to be born of a virgin. When You had overcome the sharpness of death, You opened the kingdom of heaven to all believers. You sit at the right hand of God in the glory of the Father. We believe that You will come to be our judge. We therefore pray You to help Your servants, whom You have redeemed with Your precious blood. Make them to be numbered with Your saints in glory everlasting.

O Lord, save Your people and bless Your heritage. Govern them and lift them up forever. Day by day we magnify You. And we worship Your name ever and ever. Grant, O Lord, to keep us this day without sin. O Lord, have mercy upon us, have mercy upon us. O Lord, let Your mercy be upon us, as our trust is in You. O Lord, in You have I trusted; let me never be confounded. (*LSB* pp 223–225)

NUNC DIMITTIS

Lord, now lettest Thou Thy servant depart in peace according to Thy word, for mine eyes have seen Thy salvation which Thou hast prepared before the face of all people, a light to lighten the Gentiles and the glory of Thy people Israel.

Glory be to the Father and to the Son and to the Holy Ghost; as it was in the beginning, is now, and ever shall be, world without end. Amen. (*LSB* pp. 199-200)

PRAYER PREPARING FOR WORSHIP

Dear God, You speak through Your dear Son: Blessed are those who hear Your Word. How easy it would be were we to unceasingly praise and thank You with joyful hearts that You have so benevolently and fatherly revealed Yourself to us lowly creatures, speaking with us concerning the greatest and best of all matters, namely, eternal life! You never cease to call to us through Your Son, creating in us a desire to hear Your Word, since he said: "Blessed . . . are those who hear the Word of God and keep it" (Luke 11:28)—as if You would make our ears do without it. We, who are but earth and ashes, need Your blessed Word. Oh, how unspeakably great and wondrous are Your benevolence and patience. On the other hand, affliction and woe be upon the thanklessness and stubborn blindness of those who not only refuse to hear Your Word alone but also treat it with deliberate mockery, persecution, and spite. Amen. (68)

PRAYER OF THANKSGIVING AFTER WORSHIP

O God, Father of all mercy, we thank You unceasingly that You have brought us to the treasure of Your Word through the superabundant riches of Your grace. In that Word we receive the knowledge of Your dear Son, that is, a sure deposit for our life and salvation. You have kept all those who constantly hold fast in pure faith and fervent love until the end. We thus hope and pray, merciful Father, that You would preserve us and bring us to completion with all of the elect, being of one mind, and make us to be a like image of Your dear Son, Jesus Christ, our Lord and Savior. Amen. (69)

Preparation for Holy Communion

LUTHER'S EXPLANATION OF THE SACRAMENT OF THE ALTAR*

What is the Sacrament of the Altar?

It is the true body and blood of our Lord Jesus Christ under the bread and wine, instituted by Christ Himself for us Christians to eat and to drink.

Where is this written?

The holy Evangelists Matthew, Mark, Luke, and St. Paul write:

Our Lord Jesus Christ, on the night when He was betrayed, took bread, and when He had given thanks, He broke it and gave it to the disciples and said: "Take, eat; this is My body, which is given for you. This do in remembrance of Me."

In the same way also He took the cup after supper, and when He had given thanks, He gave it to them, saying, "Drink of it, all of you; this cup is the new testament in My blood, which is shed for you for the forgiveness of sins. This do, as often as you drink it, in remembrance of Me."

What is the benefit of this eating and drinking?

These words, "Given and shed for you for the forgiveness of sins," show us that in the Sacrament forgiveness of sins, life, and salvation are given us through these words. For where there is forgiveness of sins, there is also life and salvation.

How can bodily eating and drinking do such great things?

Certainly not just eating and drinking do these things, but the words written here: "Given and shed for you for the forgiveness of sins." These words, along with the bodily eating and drinking, are the main thing in the Sacrament. Whoever believes these words has exactly what they say: "forgiveness of sins."

Who receives this sacrament worthily?

Fasting and bodily preparation are certainly fine outward training. But that person is truly worthy and well prepared who has faith in these words: "Given and shed for you for the forgiveness of sins."

But anyone who does not believe these words or doubts them is unworthy and unprepared, for the words "for you" require all hearts to believe.

*From Luther's Small Catechism.

BRIEF INSTRUCTION ON HOLY COMMUNION

Why do you intend to go to Holy Communion?

Each communicant should put that question to himself before he approaches the Table of the Lord. Many go to the Lord's Supper either quite thoughtlessly or with a wrong intention. Some go from mere force of habit; others only because their parents compel them to go; others again because they consider it a meritorious deed to partake of the Lord's Supper; still others because they wish to acquire or retain before men the appearance and name of pious Christians. It is not surprising that such communicants derive no blessing from the Holy Supper but grow worse as time goes on.

A communicant who wishes to receive the Lord's Supper to his salvation must, in the first place, fully realize what the Lord's Supper is and for what purpose it was instituted by Christ; and in the second place, he must be well prepared to receive it as a poor sinner who is yearning for forgiveness.

There are those who have an entirely wrong conception of the Holy Sacrament, who consider it merely an empty memorial, instituted only for the purpose of remembering the sufferings and death of Christ. Holy Communion is that exalted, blessed mystery by means of which Christ, in the consecrated bread, gives us His body to eat and in the consecrated wine His blood to drink. This is the very body He assumed from the Virgin Mary and gave into death on the cross for the remission of our sins. It is true, we cannot see this mystery with our eyes, taste it with our mouths, or grasp it with our minds; but we are to believe it, for our Lord and Savior says: "Take, eat; this is My body. Drink of it, all of you; this is My blood." Our Savior is faithful and true, and He will certainly bring to pass what He has promised. He is all-wise and knows ways and means to fulfill His promises, even though this is beyond our understanding. He also is almighty; with Him nothing is impossible. He is able to do exceeding abundantly above all that we ask or think. If we earnestly believe that we receive the true body and blood of our Savior—true God and man in one person—in Holy Communion, and not mere bread and wine, we shall then approach the Table of the Lord, not thoughtlessly and lightly, but in deepest reverence and humility of heart, saying as did the centurion, "Lord, . . . I am not worthy to have You come under my roof" (Luke 7:6).

The benefits derived from Holy Communion are threefold in nature. First, by worthily receiving Holy Communion we receive forgiveness of sins and the assurance that such forgiveness imparts. God, rich in love, has provided the means that poor sinners need to render them certain of the forgiveness of their sins. These means are the preaching of the Gospel, Holy Baptism, and Holy Communion. Do not be sinfully inquisitive, asking why God has instituted three means instead of one for the purpose of conveying to us the forgiveness of our sins and making us sure and certain of this, but rather thank Him for these rich provisions. He who knows from personal experience how hard it is for a soul under conviction of sin to believe that his sins are forgiven will realize the greatness of God's grace and providing care in giving us not merely one, but several means of becoming certain of the forgiveness of sin. As surely therefore as you take the Lord's body into your mouth and drink the Lord's blood, shed for the remission of your sins, so certain you are to be of having forgiveness of sins, of being the undisputed possessor of this divine gift.

The second benefit of Holy Communion is life—not the natural life we received at birth and sustain by food and drink, but the new, spiritual life that begins in regeneration through Holy Baptism. It consists of faith in our Lord Jesus Christ and the love of God and our neighbor. Our Lord has designated His Holy Supper as a spiritual nourishment for the strengthening of this spiritual life. Of this Luther writes:

> Holy Communion is aptly called a food for the soul, as it nourishes and strengthens the new man; for while we are born again by Baptism, man retains his old nature in his flesh and blood, and there are so many obstacles and temptations on the part of the devil and the world that we often grow faint and weary and at times even falter. So the Lord's Supper is given for a daily food and nourishment, that faith may be refreshed and strengthened and not repulsed in this battle, but ever grow stronger and stronger. The new life is of such a nature that it must constantly grow and progress. This new life has a great deal to endure, since the devil is an enemy who has great wrath. If he finds that he cannot take us by a bold stroke, he tries all his wiles, presents all his allurements, and does not stop until he has tired us out, so that we either abandon our faith or become listless and impatient. But when our heart is in this condition, being about to succumb, we have the comfort that in this Sacrament it can be again strengthened and refreshed.

The third benefit of Holy Communion is eternal salvation; for even as unforgiven sins bar us from heaven, so forgiveness of sins opens the door to eternal salvation. "For where there is forgiveness of sins, there is also life and salvation."

Now all depends on communing worthily and being well prepared in order to receive this threefold benefit. This, however, is not a worthiness according to the Law but according to the Gospel. It does not consist in absolute freedom from sin and perfection of life. Worthiness is realizing our unworthiness and sinfulness, in having a contrite heart that is spiritually poor, in earnestly desiring the forgiveness of sins, and in taking comfort in this forgiveness and depending solely on our Lord Jesus Christ. On the other hand, those are unworthy and ill prepared who, in their conceit of self-righteousness, fancy they need no forgiveness of sins. Consider the Pharisee, who prayed: "God, I thank You that I am not like other men" (Luke 18:11). Consider also those who wholly despair of the forgiveness of sins, as did Cain, who said: "My punishment is greater than I can bear" (Genesis 4:13), and who will not let one relieve them of their thoughts of despair. There is another class of unworthy communicant, namely, those who persist in their wicked purposes and continue to serve sin knowingly or live in a state of relentless enmity with their neighbors.

Unworthy communicants going to the Lord's Supper also receive the body and blood of Christ, but they receive it in judgment and to their great damnation. For this very purpose St. Paul adds this earnest warning: "Let a person examine himself, then, and so eat of the bread and drink of the cup. For anyone who eats and drinks without discerning the [Lord's] body eats and drinks judgment on himself" (1 Corinthians 11:28–29). Whoever recognizes in himself these marks of an unworthy communicant should not presume to go to the Lord's Table in such condition. We do not mean that he should stay away permanently, but he should immediately repent and become a truly penitent sinner.

Are those of weak faith to be classed with the unworthy communicant? Not at all. It is these very guests who are welcome and belong at Christ's Table. The Lord will surely not cast out those who are weak in faith and frail in their walk but who feel their weakness and desire to become stronger. These He invites, for it is for the weak and the frail that He instituted His Holy Supper, that they might gather strength from this spiritual food. To them He says: "Come to Me, all who labor and are heavy laden, and I will give you rest" (Matthew 11:28), and again: "Whoever comes to Me I will never cast out" (John 6:37).

CHRISTIAN QUESTIONS WITH THEIR ANSWERS*

Prepared by Dr. Martin Luther for those who intend to go to the Sacrament

After confession and instruction in the Ten Commandments, the Creed, the Lord's Prayer, and the Sacraments of Baptism and the Lord's Supper, the pastor may ask, or Christians may ask themselves these questions:

Do you believe that you are a sinner?

Yes, I believe it. I am a sinner.

How do you know this?

From the Ten Commandments, which I have not kept.

Are you sorry for your sins?

Yes, I am sorry that I have sinned against God.

What have you deserved from God because of your sins?

His wrath and displeasure, temporal death, and eternal damnation. See Romans 6:21, 23.

Do you hope to be saved?

Yes, that is my hope.

In whom then do you trust?

In my dear Lord Jesus Christ.

Who is Christ?

The Son of God, true God and man.

How many Gods are there?

Only one, but there are three persons: Father, Son, and Holy Spirit.

What has Christ done for you that you trust in Him?

He died for me and shed His blood for me on the cross for the forgiveness of sins.

Did the Father also die for you?

He did not. The Father is God only, as is the Holy Spirit; but the Son is both true God and true man. He died for me and shed His blood for me.

How do you know this?

From the holy Gospel, from the words instituting the Sacrament, and by His body and blood given me as a pledge in the Sacrament.

What are the Words of Institution?

Our Lord Jesus Christ, on the night when He was betrayed, took bread, and when He had given thanks, He broke it and gave it to the disciples and said: "Take, eat; this is My body, which is given for you. This do in remembrance of Me."

In the same way also He took the cup after supper, and when He had given thanks, He gave it to them, saying: "Drink of it, all of you; this cup is the new testament in My blood, which is shed for you for the forgiveness of sins. This do, as often as you drink it, in remembrance of Me."

Do you believe, then, that the true body and blood of Christ are in the Sacrament?

Yes, I believe it.

What convinces you to believe this?

The word of Christ: "Take, eat, this is My body; drink of it, all of you, this is My blood."

What should we do when we eat His body and drink His blood, and in this way receive His pledge?

We should remember and proclaim His death and the shedding of His blood, as He taught us: "This do, as often as you drink it, in remembrance of Me."

Why should we remember and proclaim His death?

First, so that we may learn to believe that no creature could make satisfaction for our sins. Only Christ, true God and man, could do that. Second, so we may learn to be horrified by our sins, and to regard them as very serious. Third, so we may find joy and comfort in Christ alone, and through faith in Him be saved.

What motivated Christ to die and make full payment for your sins?

His great love for His Father and for me and other sinners, as it is written in John 14; Romans 5; Galatians 2; and Ephesians 5.

Finally, why do you wish to go to the Sacrament?

That I may learn to believe that Christ, out of great love, died for my sin, and also learn from Him to love God and my neighbor.

What should admonish and encourage a Christian to receive the Sacrament frequently?

First, both the command and the promise of Christ the Lord. Second, his own pressing need, because of which the command, encouragement, and promise are given.

But what should you do if you are not aware of this need and have no hunger and thirst for the Sacrament?

To such a person no better advice can be given than this: first, he should touch his body to see if he still has flesh and blood. Then he should believe what the Scriptures say of it in Galatians 5 and Romans 7.

Second, he should look around to see whether he is still in the world, and remember that there will be no lack of sin and trouble, as the Scriptures say in John 15–16 and in 1 John 2 and 5.

Third, he will certainly have the devil also around him, who with his lying and murdering day and night will let him have no peace, within or without, as the Scriptures picture him in John 8 and 16; 1 Peter 5; Ephesians 6; and 2 Timothy 2.

Note: These questions and answers are no child's play, but are drawn up with great earnestness of purpose by the venerable and devout Dr. Luther for both young and old. Let each one pay attention and consider it a serious matter; for St. Paul writes to the Galatians in chapter six: "Do not be deceived: God cannot be mocked."

*From Luther's Small Catechism.

PRAYER BEFORE HOLY COMMUNION

Lord Jesus Christ, You call to Yourself all those who labor and are heavy burdened, to refresh them and to give rest to their souls. Dear Lord, I pray, let me also experience Your love at the heavenly feast, which You have prepared for Your children on earth. Keep me from impenitence and unbelief, so that I do not receive the Sacrament to my damnation. Remove the spotted garment of my flesh and my own righteousness, and adorn me with the garment earned by Your blood. Strengthen my faith, increase my love and hope, and hereafter make me to sit at Your heavenly table, where You give me to eat of the eternal manna and to drink of the river of Your pleasures. Hear me for Your own sake. Amen. (70)

Merciful Redeemer, You have fulfilled Your promise: "Come to me, all who labor and are heavy laden, and I will give you rest" (Matthew 11:28). At Your Table I have received nourishment for my soul, the Water of life in my weariness. By giving me, with the bread and the cup, Your body and Your blood, You have again said to me: "Fear not, for I have redeemed you; I have called you by name, you are Mine" (Isaiah 43:1). You have wiped out all my sins and have put on me the garments of Your righteousness. Make me truly grateful for Your abundant love. Let the Sacrament be in me a power overcoming unbelief and doubt, conquering temptations and evil desires, and producing good works and humble service. Having been a guest at Your Table, help me to share the Bread of life with my neighbors, so that they may share my joy and happiness. To You and the Father and the Holy Spirit be glory forever and ever. Amen. (71)

Prayers for the FESTIVALS & TIMES *of the Church Year*

Advent

O Lord Jesus Christ, King of glory, King of kings and Lord of lords, the Son of the living God and Son of David, come. Come now to Your Church that You have purchased with Your blood. Come with Your gracious presence, that we may rejoice in You. Come and rule over us, that we may serve and follow You. Come with Your love, humility, and perfect obedience, and let Your lowliness become our glory. Come into the midst of Your people and bless us, for we are Your heritage. Forgive us our sin, and do not angrily cast away Your servants, for You are meek and gracious. Clothe us with the garment of Your righteousness, for You are the only righteous one and our helper. Satisfy us with the abundance of Your mercy, for You did become poor for our sakes, that by Your poverty we might be made rich. Hear us, Lord Jesus, for the sake of Your holy name. Amen. (72)

Christmas Eve

O great and glorious Redeemer, Wonderful Counselor, Mighty God, Everlasting Father, Prince of Peace, we praise You, we bless You, we worship You, we glorify You, we give thanks to You for Your great glory. O Lord God, Lamb of God, the only begotten Son, Jesus Christ, God of God, Light of Light, very God of very God, King of kings and Lord of lords, Emmanuel, God with us! For You only are holy; You only are the Lord; You only, O Christ, with the Holy Spirit, are the most high in the glory of God the Father. But chiefly on this most holy of nights we adore You for leaving the glory that You had with the Father before the world began. We humbly ask You, by the holy mystery of Your incarnation and nativity, to deliver us, good Lord. You who came that we might have life and be saved from our sin, be gracious to us and save us. Let the glad tidings we commemorate this night be made known to all people. Amen. (73)

Christmas Day

Lord God, gracious Father, who in the fullness of time sent Your Son to become man, to assume human flesh like mine and become my Brother, I thank You for Your truth and Your fatherly goodness in giving us this Savior. By His birth, death, and resurrection, we are delivered from sin, death, Satan, and hell. I beseech You, keep me until the end in true knowledge of my Redeemer, that with the holy angels, I may rejoice at His nativity, and on the Last Day, when He comes again, I may behold Him, together with You and the Holy Spirit, in glory and majesty, world without end. Amen. (74)

New Year's Eve

Lord, make me to know my end and the measure of my days, that I may know how frail I am. Another year of my pilgrimage has passed. I am a year nearer to my death, nearer to judgment, nearer to eternal life with Christ, my Lord. Where shall I run as the sins of the past year and the transgressions of all my years rise to condemn me? Lord, to You alone I flee for refuge in these last hours of the waning year. For the sake of Your own Son, whom You sent to be the Savior of all men, be gracious to me, and pardon my iniquity. Trusting in the merits of my Savior, I come boldly to Your throne of grace, in full confidence that there I shall obtain mercy and find grace to help in time of need. Oh, satisfy me early with Your mercy that I may rejoice and be glad all my days. Let me, in a manner befitting a child of God, conclude the old year and begin the new, a year in which You would be pleased to dwell among us continually in Your goodness and means of grace; for the sake of Your dear Son, Jesus Christ, my Lord. Amen. (75)

New Year's Day

It is on account of Your mercy alone, O Lord, that I am not consumed, because Your compassions never fail. They are new every morning; great is Your faithfulness. Abide with me, O God, throughout the coming year. Be my guide in all my perplexities, my strength in my weakness, my ever-ready help in all my troubles. Forgive me all my sins. O Sabaoth Lord, look down from heaven and in grace behold and visit Your holy Church, which You have chosen for Your own. Preserve for us Your saving Word and Sacraments, that Your vine may send out its boughs from sea to sea and its branches to the uttermost parts of the earth. Look graciously upon our nation and all the nations of the world, and bless them with peace. Grant to all that are in authority wisdom and courage to rule in such a way that we may lead a quiet and peaceful life in all godliness and honesty. To You, almighty Creator and gracious God, I commit this nation, my church, my family and loved ones, and myself. Abide with me. With Your grace and mercy preserve me whole—soul and body—blameless to the coming of my Lord Jesus Christ. Amen. (76)

Epiphany

O almighty and everlasting God, who manifested Your Son, Jesus Christ, to the wise men of the East as the light to lighten the Gentiles, You have made Your only begotten Son to be both the glory of Your people Israel and the light to lighten the Gentiles. You have prepared Your salvation for all people. You have established Your Church on earth as the keeper and dispenser of the means of grace, that Your kingdom might come to all men and that Your will be done on earth as it is in heaven. I boldly ask that I be so endued with Your Holy Spirit that my joy in the Anointed One increase, that I may give glory to You, and that by all I say and do I may freely confess Your mercies among unbelievers. Let Your Church shine as holy Zion, that the Gentiles may come to her light and nations to the brightness of her rising, and that they with us and the whole host of heaven may praise You and Your most holy name, and live forever in Your presence in light and glory everlasting; through Your dear Son, our Lord and Savior, Jesus Christ. Amen. (77)

Lent

Lord Jesus, precious Savior, who went all the way to the cross to redeem me, a lost and condemned creature, graciously look upon me in this Lenten season, and let me find cleansing and healing in Your precious blood. My transgressions caused You the agony of the garden. My sins nailed You to the accursed tree. You were forsaken so that I would not be forsaken throughout all eternity. Make me see the awfulness of my sin and then Your wondrous love that would not let me die.

Grant that I may ponder day after day upon Your passion. Let nothing distracting take my thoughts from You. Draw me closer that I might find in You forgiveness and peace.

Bless this Lenten season in our many Lutheran congregations. Grant to the pastors grace to proclaim Your glorious passion with consecrated hearts, that all who hear this message of reconciliation may love You more and more. Abide with my household, and let sin have no dominion over us. As I ponder anew Your death for my transgressions, make me bold to live to You today and tomorrow and forever. Amen. (78)

Ash Wednesday

Gracious Savior, prostrate I fall at Your feet this day as Your Church once more enters the Lenten season to meditate upon Your passion, by which we have been eternally redeemed.

In spirit I appear before You in sackcloth and ashes in true repentance; let me receive Your full pardon. Do not let the pleasures of life, the worries of the day, and the activities of my daily routine crowd You out of my heart and out of my thoughts. Draw me to Your wounded side, and cleanse me with Your most precious blood. Bring healing to my soul and peace to my mind. By Your grace, let me crucify my sinful affections, lusts, and desires. Make me more than conqueror over every temptation.

I confess to You all my sins. Let none of them cling to me. Create in me a clean heart, O God, and renew a right spirit within me. Teach me to love You more and more. Give me grace to confess You as my Savior, who has redeemed me on Calvary, lifting me out of the darkness of sin to be Your own. Gracious Savior, let Your constraining love keep me and all God's children steadfast to the end. Amen. (79)

Palm Sunday

Lord Jesus, King of kings, today again I praise You with my hosannas and welcome You as the King of my heart. Enter in and take full possession of me, body, heart, mind, and soul. As thousands and ten thousands today vow faithfulness to You until death, acknowledging that they have no other Savior, grant that I, too, join this great host of faithful people to realize both the enormity and bitterness of my sin as well as the course of plenteous redemption to which You committed Yourself.

I confess, gracious Savior, that I have not been as true to You as You have been to me. Other interests have placed themselves above You in my thoughts. Have mercy upon me, and forgive me my transgressions. Sprinkle me with Your blood and wash me clean from the stain of my sin. Strengthen my heart with the assurance of my adoption and transform me according to Your image by the daily renewing of my Baptism. Preserve me in the faith until the end of days, that I may behold You in glory forevermore. Hear my cry, King of my heart and Savior of my soul. Amen. (80)

Holy Week

MONDAY

Precious Savior, Lamb of God for sinners slain, graciously forgive me all my sins, and embrace me with Your tender love. I have failed to fear, love, and trust in You above all things. This I confess, O Lord. The love of life, the allurements of the present world, the glamour of success, and the favor of friends have enticed me away from You. These things would take possession of my heart. O Lord, let me not sell my soul for the passing treasures of this present world. If I have kissed You with the kiss of betrayal, kiss me, Lord, with the kiss of forgiveness, and embrace me again as Your own. Have mercy upon me!

Protect me from the cunning of Satan, the allurements of the world, and the wickedness of my own heart. You are my surest Friend; hold me that I do not stumble and fall. Guard my heart that the love of gold, the smiles of popularity, and the eagerness to succeed may not rob me of my salvation, which You so dearly bought with Your own blood. Above all, gracious Savior, let me not despair of Your mercy, but believe at all times that Your love is as boundless as the heavens and deeper than the sea. O Friend of sinners, let me not fall away from You. Keep me standing in Your grace until I shall stand in Your presence forevermore, to love You with a perfect love throughout all eternity. Amen. (81)

TUESDAY

Lord Jesus, compassionate Savior, plead for me in the hour of trial. You know my weaknesses and shortcomings; I cannot hide my sins from You. Pray for me, gracious Redeemer, lest I deny You. O Lord, You know that I have promised to be faithful to You, and nevertheless I have again and again sinned and offended You with my many transgressions and broken pledges. I am ashamed of myself. Yet I come to You, for there is no other Savior from sin. I have denied You, if not by word, then by my actions and conduct. O Lord, look upon me in mercy, and forgive me all my sins. I have not always confessed You to the world nor spoken of the hope within me. Gracious Savior, in Your great love, forgive me. Do not let me go on in my sin. Look into my heart, and make me ashamed of myself and truly penitent.

O Lord, You know that I love You. I am Yours. Help me to be more faithful, more devout, and more zealous. In this Holy Week, lead me to a deeper appreciation of the great sacrifice that was necessary for my redemption. And, Lord, in Your mercy look upon all Your erring, sinning, straying children and bring them back and restore them to grace. Draw us all to You with Your constraining love, and keep us steadfast, unfaltering, and true. Hear my petitions and prayers. Amen. (82)

WEDNESDAY

Lord Jesus, gracious Savior, I come to You in this sacred week to ponder upon Your great and wondrous love—love that led You to the cross that my sin might be blotted out and that I might be reconciled to my heavenly Father. O Christ, give me strength and grace to crucify my sinful desires and dedicate myself anew to You, who has loved me with an everlasting love and brought to me eternal salvation. I confess to You my sins. They are many, and You know them all. For each and every one of them You suffered the agony of the cross and shed Your precious blood that I may be cleansed and made acceptable in Your sight.

Let me not go through this day unmindful of Your great love. Let none of the sins of yesterday cling to me. Humbly I come, seeking Your mercy. Daily let me fulfill the tasks and duties to which You have called me with joy, confessing You as my Lord and Savior, and being of service to my neighbor.

Grant that Your suffering and death, proclaimed for the salvation of mankind, may, by the power of the Holy Spirit, awaken in many a deeper love for You. O Lord, have mercy upon me and all sinful mankind, and create in me and all that seek You a clean heart, holy desires, and an undying love. Hear my prayer, gracious Redeemer. Amen. (83)

MAUNDY THURSDAY

Eternal Savior, how can my heart show its appreciation of Your love? How can I serve You best, who has loved me and given Your life for me? You have sealed to me the forgiveness of all my sins and offered me reconciliation and peace in the blessed Sacrament You instituted on this day. You have promised to give me, with the bread and the cup, Your body and blood for the remission of all my sins. Oh, what amazing love! What riches of divine wisdom! In awe and wonderment I ponder this gracious gift. May I ever appreciate this blessed Sacrament that You have bidden me to use as a memorial of Your death and a monument of Your redemptive love. May I come worthily each time I approach Your altar.

O Savior, cast me not away from Your presence. Let not my sins remain with me because of impenitence of heart or because I doubt Your Word and promises. Let me become one with You and all Your saints as I receive with them this blessed Sacrament. Make me Yours, and give me strength to amend my sinful life and walk closer to You.

Preserve in Your Church this blessed Sacrament, given on this sacred day. Let thousands and ten thousands find through it the assurance of forgiveness, peace, and salvation. And grant that I and all who are Yours may be faithful to Your Word and Sacraments, that Your name be glorified, Your will be done, and we at last live with You in Your eternal kingdom forevermore. Amen. (84)

GOOD FRIDAY

O Christ, Lamb of God, slain for the sin of the whole world, with penitent heart I come to Your cross, pleading for mercy and forgiveness. My sins—and they are many—have added to the burden of Your suffering and have nailed You to the accursed tree. For me You tasted the agony of the utter darkness that I might not perish, but have everlasting life. Have mercy upon me.

O Christ, Lamb of God, embrace me with Your love, and forgive me all my sins. Your death brings healing to my soul, peace to my mind, cleansing to my heart. If You would mark iniquity, I could not come, for my hands are unclean, my lips are sullied, and my heart is blackened by sin. But beholding You bleeding, despised, forsaken, dying, pierced, I come to be cleansed and forgiven.

O Christ, Lamb of God, grant that I may hate sin and wickedness more and more as I behold You in Your great agony. My grateful heart today finds hope in Your words, comfort in Your promises, and salvation in Your finished work on the cross, by which You have overcome sin, Satan, and death.

O Lord, have mercy. O Christ, have mercy. O Lord, hear my prayer. Amen. (85)

SATURDAY

Heavenly Father, I am silenced at the grave of Your Son, who knew no sin, yet was made sin for us. You permitted Him to die, exchanging His innocence for our guilt. In love He came to us, but He was rejected by hate. He taught us obedience, but men rebelled against Him.

I confess that a great mystery confronts me at this tomb of sin and death. He was buried behind the great seal of my sin and my death. By faith I know also that He who died is the One who unlocked the great secret of Your love. His tomb is my tomb. He carried with Him to the grave my sin and my death, that He might break their hold on me.

Trusting in the Lord's promise that He would rise again on the third day, I come not to mourn Him but to confess the sin that He would leave buried. Have mercy on me, O God! Have mercy on me. Amen. (86)

Easter

O almighty and eternal God, who through the death of Your Son has destroyed sin and death, and by His rising to life again restored innocence and everlasting life, that being delivered from the power of the devil, I might live under You in Your kingdom, grant that I may be forever comforted by true faith in the resurrection of Your dear Son. Do not let the thought of death fill my heart with terror, but give me the blessed assurance that, just as You raised Christ from the dead, I will not remain in the grave but will rise again at the end of days. And when, by Your grace, I have finished my course, let Christ's resurrection be for me a sure pledge that an inheritance that does not fade is reserved for me in heaven. While I live, guide me with Your holy counsel, and when I die, give me the crown of life, that with all the holy angels and the elect I may praise and glorify You, world without end. Amen. (87)

Ascension

Lord Jesus, who on the day of Your ascension withdrew Your visible body from the eyes of Your disciples, yet promised to be with them always unto the end of the world, make Your presence felt among us as we gather in Your name and around Your holy Word and Sacraments. Let these means of grace be not only Your enduring and comforting presence but also a strengthening of my faith throughout my life and to the very end of days. Remove from my heart and life the uncertainties and the doubt, the questioning and the fears brought on by the woes and chaos of the world. Strengthen my faith, that I may confidently trust Your power to save and to rule. Enable me to trust that You direct all things for good to Your Church, into which You have called me—a sheep under Your care. Above all, fill my heart with longing for that heavenly home to which You have gone to prepare a place for me, and give me a strong desire and watchful readiness for the day when I shall see You coming again to take me and all the Church into Your mansions above. In Your name I ask it. Amen. (88)

Pentecost

Holy Spirit, who on that first Pentecost established the Christian Church by Your outpouring upon the disciples in Jerusalem, I thank You that through Word and Sacrament You have continued Your Church through the ages and preserved the fellowship of the faithful throughout the years. Grant me so firm a faith in the Redeemer and so steadfast a faithfulness in Your means of grace, that through our generation You might build Your Church among the children of men. Protect us from all falsehood and error. Heal all controversy, dissension, and schism, and foster God-pleasing unity among all Christian people. Grant to me the grace to be loyal to Your Word, resisting all efforts to set aside Your revealed truth. Remove the indifference of our hearts, and make for Yourself zealous workers for Your Church, that many souls may be added to Christ's kingdom through our confession. Give to both the young and the old Your grace, that through our words and deeds we may faithfully bear witness to the Lover of our souls, and on His account, the glorious hope that lives within us; in Jesus' name. Amen. (89)

Trinity Sunday

Great triune God, Father, Son, and Holy Spirit, our Creator, Redeemer, and Sanctifier, with reverent awe and adoration I join the Church in the song of the angels: "Holy, holy, holy, is the Lord of Sabaoth. Heaven and earth are full of Your glory! Blessed is He who comes in the name of the Lord!" I praise You as the source of all blessings. In You we live and move and have our being. You have provided a sacrifice for all our sins and opened again for us the gates of paradise, which were closed to us on account of our transgressions. Through Your loving-kindness, I have not been left in the ruins of my sin; You have saved me by Your Word, washed me clean in Holy Baptism, and declared that I am a child of Your grace. And though I walk the way of Your commandments with halting steps, You daily forgive all my sins. With a grateful heart I look to You, saying: "Abba, Father." Heavenly Lord, who is one in three, grant that I may ever and always accept the mysteries of Your unerring Word, the blessings that continually come to me and all believers through the means of grace, and the privilege of my membership in the body of Christ—the Church. Give to me the joy and courage to use the talents entrusted to me as I serve my neighbor and fulfill my duty to those who depend on me. I ask this in the name of Jesus, the Author and Finisher of my faith. Amen. (90)

Reformation Festival

Lord God, who after long ages of darkness delivered the Church from the bondage of error, we thank You for those faithful witnesses through whom You restored the Gospel of Christ to men, and we praise You that this blessed light has been preserved for us to this present age. We thank You for making known among us the Holy Scriptures, which are able to make us wise unto salvation through faith in Christ Jesus, our only Mediator. Defend Your Church against all her foes. Seek and save the lost and all who have gone astray. Preserve among us the pure Word and the holy Sacraments; turn our hearts from false and pernicious doctrine. Direct and strengthen us by Your Holy Spirit that we may abide in the confession of Your Word all the days of our lives and in the end, by Your grace, obtain everlasting life. This I pray in the name of God, the Father, the Son, and the Holy Spirit. Amen. (91)

Day of Humiliation and Prayer

O great God, just and holy, I, a sinful, unclean creature, come before You in deep humility, confessing my many sins and my total unworthiness. Enter not into judgment against Your servant, for in Your sight no man living shall be justified. Have mercy upon me, O God, according to Your loving-kindness; according to the multitude of Your tender mercies, blot out my transgressions. I am aware of my many failings and that I deserve nothing but Your displeasure and punishment. But heavenly Father, You are loving and merciful. Though my sins be as scarlet, make them white as snow. In the wounds of Jesus You have provided cleansing for my uncleanness and pardon for my iniquity. Through Your Holy Spirit let me take refuge at all times in the sacred wounds of my Savior and put my trust in His atoning sacrifice. Pardoned by You, strengthened through Your Word and Sacraments, show me how I can go out with a joyful heart, eager to serve You in my work and in service to my family and neighbors. Hear me for the sake of my precious Redeemer, Jesus Christ. Amen. (92)

Prayers for the
CHURCH & HER WORK

FOR THE CHURCH AT LARGE

Lord Jesus Christ, in this world of unrest and strife You founded Your holy Christian Church through faith as a kingdom of peace and joy. You have established this worldwide communion of saints in which all believers are joined by the invisible bond of faith and in which we are gathered around Your Word and Sacraments. I thank You for making me a citizen in Your holy kingdom through the cleansing waters of Baptism. I praise You for Your goodness because You bestowed upon me and all Your children Your Holy Spirit. Keep the flame of faith alive in all believers through the forgiveness and peace given us through Your precious body and blood in the bread and wine of the Sacrament. Continue to fill us with the spirit of love and peace toward one another. Make us the salt of the earth and the light of the world. Fulfill among us Your promise that the gates of hell shall not prevail against Your Church. Extend Your kingdom so that Your salvation reaches to the ends of the earth. Hear us for the sake of Your truth. Amen. (93)

FOR THE LEADERS OF OUR SYNOD

O Lord, God and Father, send the bright beams of Your grace and mercy on the leaders of our synod, as they serve the people of our church. Equip them with every good and perfect gift that comes down from above. Give them wisdom and insight, that they may discern what is best as they provide national leadership of our church. Give them courage and strength as they deal with pressing and difficult issues of church administration and supervision. Most of all, keep them faithful to their promise to carry out their office according to Your holy Word and in accord with the Lutheran Confessions. Do not let the stresses and pressures and difficulties of their office discourage them or lead them into error. Keep far from them the temptations of the evil one. Give them the heart of the Good Shepherd, that they may serve You and Your people with humility, so that in all they do, they may decrease, so that the kingdom of Christ may increase. Let them stand without wavering on Your clear and gracious Word. By the infallible truth and power of Christ and Him crucified, let them be comforted in all the difficulties that their office brings. By the power of Your Spirit, give them peace and joy in their service to You, and make them a blessing to our church, as together we give You all praise, honor, and glory, O Father, together with the Son and the Holy Spirit, one God, forever and ever. Amen. (94)

FOR THE INCREASE OF THE CHURCH IN ALL NATIONS

Our Father in heaven, who gave Your only begotten Son, our Lord Jesus, into death for the sins of the whole world, look with compassion on the many millions of sinners who yet sit in darkness and the shadow of eternal death. Send messengers to proclaim Your Word in the benighted corners of this earth where it has not been heard. Strengthen Your Church where she is weak or persecuted. Send teachers to reform her where she is in error. Raise up pastors in every nation under heaven. Bless those in every land who baptize and teach in Your name. Defend them from all evil, give them a rich measure of Your peace and joy, and enable them to speak Your Word with boldness. Open doors for the Gospel, and empower by

Your Holy Spirit those who hear it to believe it and be saved. Let the hordes of Satan not prevail against Your Church or snatch the seed of Your Word from people's hearts. Call out of darkness into Your marvelous light a kingdom of priests and a holy nation from every nation, tribe, people, and language, that many may share in the eternal banquet You have prepared for those who have washed their robes and made them white in the blood of the Lamb. For His sake we are bold to come before Your throne of grace, trusting in Your mercy. Amen. (95)

FOR OUR COLLEGES AND SEMINARIES

Dear Lord, You have given Your Word as a light to a sin-sick world, and by that Word You bless us with salvation. You have raised up for Yourself the seminaries and universities of the Church, where Your children are gathered and trained to do Your will and further Your kingdom here on earth. Be with those studying to be pastors and teachers in the Church. Open for their learning the life-giving Scriptures, and keep them faithful and focused in their studies. Give them the skill and confidence to confess You as Savior even as they teach others of Your salvation. Grant those men and women preparing for vocations in the Church the strength needed to keep their eyes focused on their studies. Help them through the temptations the devil will use to distract and discourage them. When stress and doubts appear, speak to them through Your Word and Sacrament the comforting promise of peace with You in this world and eternal rest in the next. Keep students and instructors humble, receiving Your Word with a childlike faith, so that in all they say and do, the light of Your Word is focused and bright. Give the instructors in our seminaries and universities not only knowledge but also the ability to share this knowledge and pass on our Christian heritage. Give the instructors a Christlike care and compassion for their students. Grant the students willing and open minds to receive this instruction, that they may be formed by Your Word and become leaders in the Church, sharing the life-giving Gospel of Jesus Christ, who died and rose to save us all; in His name. Amen. (96)

FOR THE CONGREGATION

Dearest Jesus, my Redeemer and the Shepherd of my soul, I thank You that through Holy Baptism You have made me a member of Your body, the Church. I entreat You to bless most richly the congregation of saints of which You have called me to be a part. May Your Word always be purely preached and taught among us, and may we gladly hear and learn it and grow in knowledge of and love for You. May Your Sacraments be given according to Your command, and may we always value most highly the forgiveness of sins and eternal life You give us through them. Work in us love and respect for our pastor. Help us to uphold him and his family in prayer and obey him as Your undershepherd, so that with joy he may fulfill the task You have given him of guarding our souls. Prepare us through his ministry to use the gifts You have given each of us in service to others, that Your body might be built up. Keep far from us pride and dissension. Help us, without jealousy, to value the diverse gifts You have given our brothers and sisters. Teach us to weep with and support those who suffer and to rejoice with those who rejoice. Call, gather, and enlighten many others to travel with us on the journey to heaven, where You together with the Father and the Holy Spirit are worshiped by saints and angels, now and forever. Amen. (97)

FOR THE LUTHERAN DAY SCHOOL

Jesus, Savior and Good Shepherd, who has given Your life to save us, You have directed us to feed and tend Your lambs and sheep. Bless our Lutheran schools. Strengthen, equip, and encourage all who teach and all who learn in them, so that Your name is praised and honored as knowledge, skills, and attitudes are imparted and acquired. Make our school a haven of Your grace and mercy. Give patience and discernment to our teachers as they daily interact with their students. Give them the insight to apply rightly both Law and Gospel, equipping their students to share the Good News of the forgiveness of sins won for us on Calvary.

As Your holy Word is studied, applied, and committed to memory by our students, cause it to find fertile soil that it may bear fruit in a greater understanding of You and in a genuine appreciation of Your saving and preserving means of grace. Establish our school as a blessing to our students and families, to our entire congregation, and to our community. Through Word and Sacrament, strengthen and encourage each of our school families so they grow in faith toward You and in love to one another, that, by Your grace, they may be a light in a world held captive in the darkness of sin. Amen. (98)

FOR THE SUNDAY SCHOOL

Lord Jesus, our Savior and Redeemer, You have given the Church the command to bring the children to You that they may find hope in the promise of everlasting life with You. Therefore, help and support our pastor(s) and leaders as they assist our parents in nurturing the baptismal faith of Your little lambs. You alone can preserve them in faith against all the evil influences of this world, yet You have given to us the task, the privilege, and the means to nurture the faith of all our children. You alone can create faith and hope and love in these children, yet You call men and women to teach Your holy Word. I thank and praise You for such grace and compassion. Bless the instruction offered in our Sunday school. May Your Word nourish and sustain all who hear it. Bring all teachers to realize not only the importance of their vocation but also that You promise to be with them and that they, too, are children of God redeemed with Your holy, precious blood. Give them the wisdom, understanding, and ability to proclaim to the children entrusted to their care the truths of Your Word that provides the certainty of the salvation You have won for them. May the lives of our teachers so agree with Your instruction that they may always be shining examples of Christian virtue among us. I ask You to hear my prayer for Your sake. Amen. (99)

FOR OUR PASTOR(S)

Lord Jesus, You are my great High Priest, who intercedes with the Father on my behalf. During Your earthly ministry You called men to be Your apostles, and still today You call men to be pastors in Your Church—to proclaim the Gospel of the forgiveness of sins, to baptize, to nourish Your people with Your holy Supper, and to minister in countless ways to Your flock.

Grant to my pastor(s) fidelity to Your Word, wisdom by Your Spirit, and strength from above, that he may carry out his calling faithfully. Make him a fearless confessor of Your truth. Keep him from error in his teaching and from scandal in his life. Give him courage to admonish those who stray, compassion to bind up the brokenhearted, and discernment to apply Law and Gospel to all appropriately. May he protect Your flock from ravaging wolves and shepherd Your lambs into green pastures.

Move the members of my congregation to have proper respect for our pastor(s), to obey him, and to gladly accept the Word preached to us. Keep our pastor(s) and our parishioners faithful until death, that together we may receive the crown of life; in Your name, O Jesus, the only Savior of the world. Amen. (100)

FOR OUR TEACHERS

Lord God, heavenly Father, You sent Your Son, Jesus, to this sinful world to save us from our sinfulness. He lived a perfect life for us and gave us the perfect example of a master teacher. Thank You for the gift of faithful teachers who explain the Word to the children and adults entrusted to their care, leading them to knowledge of Your truth. You have called them to serve You in Your kingdom, and You alone empower them with all the gifts they need in their blessed vocation. Lord, continue to bless Your Church with faithful, dedicated teachers who seek to give You all glory in their vocation for the work You do through them. Fill them with the fervent desire to do that which is pleasing in Your eyes: to do Your will, to walk in Your ways, and to extol Your means of grace. Guard them from any error in judgment, word, or deed. Give them patience in dealing with the challenges of their classrooms. Bring to their remembrance and support them with the promise of Your presence in every aspect of their life and vocation. May our teachers find true joy, comfort, and peace in Your enduring Gospel as You sustain them in their work; in the name of our dear Lord Jesus. Amen. (101)

FOR DEACONESSES AND THE MINISTRY OF MERCY

O eternal God, who mercifully gives us all things for this body and life, granting us eternal mercy through Your Son, Jesus, who fed the hungry, healed the sick, comforted the grieving, and befriended the outcast, make us mindful of Your care through the lives and service of those who have been called to works of mercy in Your name on behalf of Your Church. We especially implore You to strengthen and aid the service of deaconesses and all those who act as Your hands of mercy unto the least of these. Grant them perseverance in their vocation and courage to hold forth the Gospel as they bring aid and comfort to those in need. Bless us, Your saints, who by faith in Christ Jesus reach out in mercy to our neighbors. Let Your Holy Spirit consecrate our efforts through Your mercy, which finds its fulfillment in the cross of Christ, that we may worthily serve You in the works of mercy You have given us to do, to Your glory and the praise of Your Son, Jesus Christ, and the Holy Spirit forever. Amen. (102)

FOR MISSIONS AT HOME

Great God, Father, Son, and Holy Spirit, You desire that all people be baptized and saved from eternal death. You do not desire the death of one transgressor, but that sinners should turn from their evil ways and live with You in eternity. I humbly ask You to remember in mercy and love the unbelievers in this land of ours. Remember those who have never heard the way of salvation, and lead them to the knowledge of the truth of Jesus Christ. Grant that the messengers of Your Gospel may reach many and bring them the sweet tidings of Your redeeming grace. Let the Spirit of truth work through the Holy Scriptures to bring the forgiveness of sins to the lost. I commend Your messengers to Your heavenly protection, and I ask You to make powerful the Word they proclaim to those who are outside of the faith. Gather the lost into the fold of the Good Shepherd of our souls. I ask this in the name of our blessed Redeemer, Jesus Christ. Amen. (103)

Table of Duties

*Certain passages of Scripture for various offices and positions, admonishing them about their vocation and duties, drawn together by Dr. Martin Luther**

TO BISHOPS, PASTORS, AND PREACHERS

The overseer must be above reproach, the husband of but one wife, temperate, self-controlled, respectable, hospitable, able to teach, not given to drunkenness, not violent but gentle, not quarrelsome, not a lover of money. He must manage his own family well and see that his children obey him with proper respect (1 Timothy 3:2–4). He must not be a recent convert, or he may become conceited and fall under the same judgment as the devil (1 Timothy 3:6). He must hold firmly to the trustworthy message as it has been taught, so that he can encourage others by sound doctrine and refute those who oppose it (Titus 1:9).

WHAT THE HEARERS OWE THEIR PASTORS

The Lord has commanded that those who preach the gospel should receive their living from the gospel (1 Corinthians 9:14). Anyone who receives instruction in the word must share all good things with his instructor. Do not be deceived: God cannot be mocked. A man reaps what he sows (Galatians 6:6–7). The elders who direct the affairs of the church well are worthy of double honor, especially those whose work is preaching and teaching. For the Scripture says, "Do not muzzle the ox while it is treading out the grain," and "The worker deserves his wages" (1 Timothy 5:17–18).

We ask you, brothers, to respect those who work hard among you, who are over you in the Lord and who admonish you. Hold them in the highest regard in love because of their work. Live in peace with each other (1 Thessalonians 5:12–13). Obey your leaders and submit to their authority. They keep watch over you as men who must give an account. Obey them so that their work will be a joy, not a burden, for that would be of no advantage to you (Hebrews 13:17).

OF CIVIL GOVERNMENT

Everyone must submit himself to the governing authorities, for there is no authority except that which God has established. The authorities that exist have been established by God. Consequently, he who rebels against the authority is rebelling against what God has instituted, and those who do so will bring judgment on themselves. For rulers hold no terror for those who do right, but for those who do wrong. Do you want to be free from fear of the one in authority? Then do what is right and he will commend you. For he is God's servant to do you good. But if you do wrong, be afraid, for he does not bear the sword for nothing. He is God's servant, an agent of wrath to bring punishment on the wrongdoer (Romans 13:1–4).

OF CITIZENS

Give to Caesar what is Caesar's, and to God what is God's (Matthew 22:21). It is necessary to submit to the authorities, not only because of possible punishment but also because of conscience. This is also why you pay taxes, for the authorities are God's servants, who give their full time to governing. Give everyone what you owe him: If you owe taxes, pay taxes; if revenue, then revenue; if respect, then respect; if honor, then honor (Romans 13:5–7). I urge, then, first of all, that requests, prayers, intercession and thanksgiving be made for everyone—for kings and all those in authority, that we may live peaceful and quiet lives in all godliness and holiness. This is good, and pleases God our Savior (1 Timothy 2:1–3).

Remind the people to be subject to rulers and authorities, to be obedient, to be ready to do whatever is good (Titus 3:1). Submit yourselves for the Lord's sake to every authority instituted among men: whether to the king, as the supreme authority, or to governors, who are sent by Him to punish those who do wrong and to commend those who do right (1 Peter 2:13–14).

TO HUSBANDS

Husbands, in the same way be considerate as you live with your wives, and treat them with respect as the weaker partner and as heirs with you of the gracious gift of life, so that nothing will hinder your prayers (1 Peter 3:7). Husbands, love your wives and do not be harsh with them (Colossians 3:19).

TO WIVES

Wives, submit to your husbands as to the Lord (Ephesians 5:22). They were submissive to their own husbands, like Sarah, who obeyed Abraham and called him her master. You are her daughters if you do what is right and do not give way to fear (1 Peter 3:5–6).

TO PARENTS

Fathers, do not exasperate your children; instead, bring them up in the training and instruction of the Lord (Ephesians 6:4).

TO CHILDREN

Children, obey your parents in the Lord, for this is right. "Honor your father and your mother"—which is the first commandment with a promise—"that it may go well with you and that you may enjoy long life on the earth" (Ephesians 6:1–3).

TO WORKERS OF ALL KINDS

Slaves, obey your earthly masters with respect and fear, and with sincerity of heart, just as you would obey Christ. Obey them not only to win their favor when their eye is on you, but like slaves of Christ, doing the will of God from your heart. Serve wholeheartedly, as if you were serving the Lord, not men, because you know that the Lord will reward everyone for whatever good he does, whether he is slave or free (Ephesians 6:5–8).

TO EMPLOYERS AND SUPERVISORS

Masters, treat your slaves in the same way. Do not threaten them, since you know that he who is both their Master and yours is in heaven, and there is no favoritism with Him (Ephesians 6:9).

TO YOUTH

Young men, in the same way be submissive to those who are older. All of you, clothe yourselves with humility toward one another, because, "God opposes the proud but gives grace to the humble." Humble yourselves, therefore, under God's mighty hand, that He may lift you up in due time (1 Peter 5:5–6).

TO WIDOWS

The widow who is really in need and left all alone puts her hope in God and continues night and day to pray and to ask God for help. But the widow who lives for pleasure is dead even while she lives (1 Timothy 5:5–6).

TO EVERYONE

The commandments . . . are summed up in this one rule: "Love your neighbor as yourself" (Romans 13:9).

I urge . . . that requests, prayers, intercession and thanksgiving be made for everyone (1 Timothy 2:1).

Let each his lesson learn with care,
and all the household well shall fare.

*From Luther's Small Catechism.

Prayers Concerning
CHRISTIAN VOCATION

Prayers for Our World, Nation, and Community

FOR PEACE

Heavenly Father, God of peace and harmony, You would have Your children on earth live together in peace and quietness. Frustrate the plans of all evil men who would stir up violence and strife; spoil the weapons of those who delight in war and bloodshed; and according to Your will, end all wars in the world. Lead us to confess the truth of Your Word that from the lusts of our own hearts come wars and fighting among us. Help me by Your Word and Spirit to crucify my sinful flesh and to root out the evil that would lead to strife and discord, so that to the best of my ability, I may be at peace with my neighbor. Mercifully hear my prayer and grant us peace in our days. In Jesus' name I pray. Amen. (104)

AT THE OUTBREAK OF ARMED CONFLICT OR WAR

Almighty God, I love peace and yet I now find that my country is entering into armed conflict. I know that wars come because we, Your creatures, are sinners, among whom I am chief. Grant us forgiveness and repentance for our part in failing to keep the peace. You, O Lord, make wars cease to the ends of the earth. You break the bow and shatter the spear and burn the chariots in the fire. Grant a speedy end to this conflict. May the horrors of war move the world's leaders to find a just and lasting solution to the things that now separate us. War so easily spirals out of control. So, check the hatred and cruelty of war; watch over the children and all innocent parties; and moderate all human behavior. Instill in us all an abhorrence of war that will make us all work tirelessly to find peaceful ways to solve our world's problems. May this war, and all rumors of war, remind me that Jesus Christ, my Lord and Savior, will soon return to bring His kingdom of peace to all who believe in Him. Amen. (105)

AT A TIME OF NATIONAL CRISIS OR CALAMITY

Heavenly Father, I come to Your throne of mercy, bowed down and wearied by the weight of suffering and disaster visited upon our country. I beg You to protect this nation in our hour of need. I acknowledge my trespasses before You and do not deny either my own transgressions of Your holy Law or the sins of other citizens of my homeland. We are laden with iniquity, but You call us to Your forgiveness, salvation, hope, and life. Turn the hearts and minds of all to You, that they might find peace through the cleansing of Jesus' blood. Let me not be confounded or dismayed, so that I, a child of Your grace, may courageously speak to this needy world of the hope that is within me. Make me an instrument of Your peace in a world of conflict, a witness to the power of faith in a world lost in unbelief, and a bearer of the joy that overcomes the sorrow of a fallen world. Grant to the leaders of this nation and all the nations of the world wise counsel, calm thinking, and unselfish aims. Amid the tumult of disaster, build Your kingdom and turn even more souls to Yourself. Because of Your grace, we are not altogether lost but find peace and forgiveness in

You. O Lord, give me the grace to seek You, trust You, and confess You; in Jesus' name. Amen. (106)

AT A TIME OF NATIONAL PROSPERITY

O Father of lights, from whom all good and perfect gifts do proceed, I thank You that You have graciously provided all that I need to preserve this body and life. May I receive and use these gifts with joy, O Lord, for without Your blessing even wealth is poverty. May I never have so much that I forget You, and may I never have so little that by want of daily bread I despair of Your goodness. As You have been generous with our land, may we be liberal in our giving to others, for truly it is more blessed to give than to receive. I pray, good Lord, that my faith may never be in uncertain riches, but in You, the living God. For by the resurrection of Christ our Lord from the dead, You have defeated the death of sin in me and have given me glorious life in Your own heavenly home, where the streets are paved with gold. Be merciful and kind to those who are in want. Give employment and encouragement to all people. Strengthen all in their appropriate callings, by which You produce earthly riches. All this I ask through Christ Jesus, my dear Lord. Amen. (107)

FOR THE DEFENSE OF OUR COUNTRY

O almighty, everlasting, loving, and protective Father, I humbly come before You to ask that Your protective arms enfold me and the citizens of this nation. As we live our lives, we daily hear about the tragic results of war and the threats that are uttered against our nation and against us. I beg You, dear Father, to hear my prayers as You have promised and calm my fearful and trembling heart and mind. Everyday, I hear and read of threats to the security and the stability of this nation. As You have said, there will always be threats of war and rumors of war. We also now hear the threat of attack of every form and of every kind upon our children and upon us. These threats, these rumors, and these acts of evil cause me to be afraid. Lord, I pray that You would not allow me to be confused or confounded by those who promote terror and massive destruction and harm upon Your people. But I pray that You would, through the Holy Spirit, increase and strengthen my faith, that I would always turn to You, my refuge and my strength. Be with those whom You have raised up to serve and protect us. Grant them the resolve and the commitment to perform their duties so as to promote peace and safety and security for me as well as for all my fellow citizens. I pray, dear Father, that You and Your holy angels would defend us from attack, confound those who would deprive us of our freedom, and thwart the evil efforts of those who intend to cause pain, suffering, and death by their cowardly acts of assassination, humiliation, intimidation, murder, and fear.

Dear heavenly Father, You have promised to love, to protect, and to provide for Your people. If it be according to Your holy will, keep me safe in a world that is far from safe, faithful in a world that knows little of true faith, and secure in this world that knows no real security apart from You, until that time that You call me to be with You for all eternity. I boldly ask these blessings in the holy name of Christ Jesus, my Lord and my Savior. Amen. (108)

FOR OUR ARMED FORCES

O Creator of the universe, You did not form Adam from the dust of the world so that his children would spill their brothers' blood in that dust. With Adam's sin came death, destruction, and war. Yet You did not turn from Your fallen creation but embraced it in the flesh of Your incarnate Son, winning our peace with You though His death and resurrection. Still, humanity rebels, and evil flourishes with wars and rumors of war. Young men and women today protect our nation in the profession of arms, even now serving in places of danger, to shield us from the manifested evil of terrorism, weapons of mass destruction, and other wicked instruments of Satan's hatred. I pray, dear Lord of peace, that You would protect those who wear the uniform of my country and serve with courage, honor, and commitment. Comfort and strengthen our sailors, marines, soldiers, airmen, and coast guardsmen. Be with their loved ones who must wait at home while they go to far and distant lands, answering the call of duty. Bless the faithful ministry of chaplains who go with them to proclaim Your Gospel and administer Your Sacraments on ships and in foxholes. Guide the leaders of this world that they may seek to walk in peace so that the skills of warriors may not be used except to deter those who would seek to harm us. I ask this in the name of the Prince of Peace, the only Savior of the world, Jesus the Christ. Amen. (109)

ON INDEPENDENCE DAY

Eternal Father, Ruler of all nations, on this day when my country celebrates its birth, I thank You for all spiritual and temporal blessings enjoyed in our land. In Your mercy, You have sustained this nation in times of trouble and preserved its liberties. Teach me anew to treasure especially that dearly won freedom of conscience and worship that is the cornerstone of this country's principles. Let me not misuse this liberty nor forget that true freedom is freedom to serve. Give me willingness to share in the process of democratic rule, to respect my country's laws, and to work for the preservation of its institutions. Forgive our past sins committed as a nation in the name of misguided patriotism, self-interest, or political expediency. Confound all those who, for the sake of partisanship or other motives, would sacrifice the greater welfare. Grant wisdom to our leaders. Strengthen all those who strive to do Your will. Increase loyalty to You and to our beloved country. Protect me and my fellow citizens from all subversive or terrorist acts. Above all, dear God, speed the course of Your Gospel among us, so that by the power of the Holy Spirit, hearts are turned to that freedom from sin and death that You alone graciously give through Jesus Christ. Amen. (110)

ON MEMORIAL DAY

Gracious Lord, heavenly Father, on this day we pause to remember the sacrifices made for freedom throughout the past centuries. We do indeed owe a debt of gratitude to those who have paid dearly for the liberty we enjoy. Yet, O Lord, I know that good government, peace, and freedom are really gifts granted from Your fatherly hand, as I confess in the Creed. As we remember those who have served our nation, help us to remember that civic duty, no matter how well done, does not grant entrance to Your kingdom. We are saved by grace, through faith in Christ, apart from our works. Freed from the Law's demands, I know that I am now free to serve my neighbor for my neighbor's sake. May the sacrifices of those who have gone before me serve as examples. When I meet those who have served, remind me to thank them. Almighty God, guide the leaders of our nation. Watch over those who serve in our armed forces, especially those far from home. And above all, grant that we, Your children by faith in Christ, may find a field of service in which we, as salt and leaven, may uphold righteousness, order, and peace; in Jesus' name. Amen. (111)

ON VETERANS DAY

O Lord, I remember on this day the horrors of war and the mercies of Your providence in the past. I give You thanks for those who have served in our armed forces and the families that have loved them, missed their presence, interceded in prayer for them, and rejoiced in their return. Especially, though, I pray for those families who did not see their loved ones return because they gave their lives in defense of freedom and this land that I love. May I never forget the sacrifices that have been made for me by these courageous men and women. Lord of the nations, I pray, according to Your good and gracious will, that You would grant peace among nations in this time as well. Put into the hearts of rulers and nations the desire to avert bloodshed, strife, and selfishness, and cause all to see the folly of war. You guarantee to all eternal peace in Christ. May Your Gospel be proclaimed that the foundation of love may be laid in Christ Jesus, the Prince of Peace. In His name I ask it. Amen. (112)

ON THANKSGIVING DAY

Oh, give thanks to the Lord, for He is good and His mercy endures forever. Lord God, heavenly Father, You have created me and endowed me with all that I am or have as a pure gift of Your "fatherly, divine goodness and mercy, without any merit or worthiness in me." You sustain me from day to day with the gifts of daily bread in the food that I eat, the family that surrounds me, the friends I enjoy, the country where I live, and countless other benefits that I constantly receive from Your open hand. On this Day of Thanksgiving, cause me to gratefully remember the good gifts that You shower upon me. Deepen in me the knowledge of Your goodness, and awaken my heart to praise You for all of Your gifts, especially the forgiveness of sins that You have purchased and won for me and the whole world in the atoning death of Your Son, Jesus Christ. Keep me mindful of Your mercies every day, and grant that I may thank, praise, serve, and obey You not only with my lips but also with a life dedicated to the service of my neighbor. To You, O Lord, Father, Son, and Holy Spirit, be all honor and glory, praise and thanksgiving, now and forever. Amen. (113)

FOR GOVERNMENT

Lord God, as I pray for all who are in authority, I thank You especially for the form of government given us in our beloved country. Give me the grace with my fellow citizens to value the officers and the magistrates of our government as those sent by You. Instill in me that respect and honor that is due them. Lord, endow them with wisdom for their several duties, with a spirit of sacrifice for the common welfare, with mercy and justice, with uprightness and kindliness. Correct the evils of selfishness, greed, a vain desire for honor, or abuse of power among us as well as in the other governments of the world. Grant that the true purposes of government may prevail, safeguarding peace and prosperity, so that we may live soberly and uprightly in Your sight and have opportunity to tell of You and Your kingdom. These petitions I direct to You because in Jesus I know You as my Father and Lord. Amen. (114)

FOR PUBLIC SAFETY ORGANIZATIONS AND WORKERS

In accordance with Your Word, O God, my Savior, hear the prayers I pray for all those in authority. As You have ordained these powers so that I might live a quiet, peaceable, and godly life in this present age, prosper them in their blessed vocation as police, fire, and emergency medical officers. As they protect, protect them, O Lord, from all harm and danger. Keep them safe in their work. Give them success in preserving the life and property that You have graciously given to us. May they find joy in performing the service You have given them to do. May they be ever mindful of Your presence with them, even in their darkest hour. Comfort their loved ones who share them with us and who weep when they weep. When they are weak, give them strength. When they are afraid, give them courage. When they are in doubt, grant them wisdom from above. When they have sinned, grant them repentance and true faith in Christ, who made the ultimate sacrifice in order to save us all from sin and eternal death. Grant them the peace of Christ. Amen. (115)

FOR FIELDS AND CROPS

Bounteous God, we praise Your power and majesty which You have revealed in the growing things of Your creation on land and in the sea. Teach me, dear Lord, to know that in due season You supply daily bread for us and all mankind. Banish from our hearts all selfishness, all pride. Give us the needed diligence and necessary skill in the sowing and gathering of our harvests. Protect our fields from pestilence, hail, fire, and floods, and let the earth yield its increase. If it be Your good will, grant peace and prosperity to the nation, that each one may find sufficient bread for his daily need. Quicken our hearts to share with the needy wherever they may be. Make us a thankful people as we enjoy working amid growing things, and open our eyes to behold the beauty of Your creation. Teach us to seek first Your kingdom and Your righteousness, and then add the necessary food and protection for today. Grant that the fruits of the field may find their way to those who are most in need, according to Your grace. These gifts I ask of You because You are the giver of all things we need for body and for soul. Amen. (116)

IN A STORM OR NATURAL DISASTER

Heavenly Father, I know Your greatness and my weakness, Your majesty and my unworthiness. By this present storm (disaster), You call us to the knowledge of our sin and to true repentance, lest we forget Your just judgment against sin. Do not let us be condemned with this wicked and evil world. O Lord, I am helpless and need Your protection. For Jesus' sake abide with me. Lift up Your face and be gracious to me in this fearful time of danger, and do not test me beyond my strength. Protect my home and my dear ones, especially those who are weak and helpless. Send Your holy angel, that I may continue safely to my journey's end. Give me faith to cast my anxieties and cares on You, who stills storms and guides the souls of men through every danger; in Jesus' name. Amen. (117)

Prayers for Our Neighbors, Our Family, and Ourselves

ON ONE'S BIRTHDAY

My Lord and my God, in You alone I live and move and have my being. Today I again mark the day of my birth and the beginning of my temporal life. In deep gratitude I also recall my spiritual birth in the waters of Holy Baptism as You reconciled me to Yourself and cleansed me of my sin. For all this I thank and praise You. This day reminds me, to Your praise, O God, my Creator, that I was not only born into this world, but also that You have bought me to a place where Your name is truly known, Your Word is taught in purity, and where, by Your means of grace, true faith is kindled. I thank You for the benefits that You have showered upon me, both for my life here and for my life yet to come, from the day of my birth to this very hour. You have nourished and kept me. By Your holy angels, You have protected my life in ways I can hardly imagine, and You have provided my bodily needs of food, clothing, and shelter in rich measure. To this grace upon grace You have added Your Word, through which You deliver forgiveness, comfort, and peace for each day of my life. How wonderful are the works of Your hands, O Lord, and Your mercy rich beyond measure!

Let me ever be mindful of my sinful beginning and my well-deserved punishment. But You have sought me out, the lost sheep; You have redeemed me, sanctified me, comforted me, governed me, and preserved me in my calling. Daily grant me forgiveness of sins as well as steadfastness in saving faith all the days You have prepared in advance for me, that I may serve You in true faith. In Jesus' name I pray. Amen. (118)

FOR STRONGER FAITH

Lord Jesus, I believe. Help my unbelief! Strengthen my weak and flickering faith. I know that You are my wisdom, my righteousness, my sanctification, and my redemption. Lord, strengthen this faith in me, that I may never fear nor faint in any trial or temptation. You alone are the Author and Finisher of my faith. Though my faith be tried with fire, may I ever be found strong and unmovable to the glory of Your holy name.

Let me firmly trust in Your blood, which cleanses me from all sin, that though my sins are as scarlet, they shall be as white as snow. When I am enticed by sin and the world beckons and my own passions want to yield, help my unbelief, and give me the strength and will to resist. When trials, sorrow, and affliction want to rob me of this trust, O Lord, help me to remain steadfast and true. Strengthen my faith in Your promise that all things work together for good to them that love God, to them that are called according to Your purpose to be Your own here in time and there in eternity. You, O almighty Lord, can help; You, O gracious Lord, will help my unbelief; You, O merciful Lord, will strengthen my faith. Lord, I believe! Amen. (119)

TO LIVE A HOLY LIFE

Lord Jesus, by Your precious blood You redeemed me, a lost and condemned creature, and called me to be Your very own, a fellow citizen with the saints. You, O Lord, know all things. You know that I love You. You know that my renewed heart desires to serve You in righteousness and holiness, to cast aside the sin that so easily entangles me, and to run with perseverance the race set before me. I grieve, O Lord, that I have so often failed to do what You, my precious Savior, have asked me. So often I have refused to follow You and Your example, instead choosing the paths of the world and the desires of my sinful flesh. In me there is no good thing. The good that I would do, I do not; and the evil that I would not, that I do. I am so wretched! Who will deliver me from this body of death? To You, my Savior and loving Friend, I flee. Uphold me with Your willing Spirit. You are the Author and Perfecter of my faith, having delivered me from the guilt and punishment of sin and having redeemed me from its power and dominion. Create in me a clean heart, O God, and renew a right spirit within me. Purge every evil desire and thought from my heart and mind, and fill me with a pure love for You and Your will. Whether I live or die, may I be Yours alone and forever. Amen. (120)

OF HUSBAND AND WIFE

Our Lord Jesus Christ, You are the Bridegroom of the Church, Your holy bride. In Your name we have been united as husband and wife in holy wedlock that we may walk hand in hand until this life ends. Make our hearts temples of Your Spirit, that we may live with undying gratitude that for our salvation You became incarnate, suffered death on the cross, rose from the grave, and ascended into heaven, where even now You intercede for us with God the Father.

Fill our marriage with Your sacrificial love. Give us children if it be Your will, and enable us to raise them with faith in You. Grant that we daily trust in Your grace. Forgive us our sins, as we forgive one another. As You are merciful and kind, slow to anger and abounding in mercy, help us so to be. May the Holy Spirit yield in us the fruit of love, joy, peace, patience, kindness, gentleness, and self-control.

Since we have become one flesh, help us protect this union in exclusive fidelity and keep it sacred. When faced with temptation, give us courage to remain faithful and reject sin. May Your holy Word guide, instruct, and comfort us in all circumstances, that harmoniously together we may arrive at God-pleasing decisions for life's many challenges. With expectant hope we await Your return in glory, whereupon the everlasting wedding feast shall commence. In Your most precious and saving name we pray, O Lord Jesus Christ. Amen. (121)

ON THE DAY OF A WEDDING ANNIVERSARY

Almighty God, You created marriage as an honorable estate that gives us a picture of the very communion of Christ and His bride, the Church. The union of husband and wife in body and soul provides help, comfort, and mutual joy—in times of adversity and suffering as well as in prosperity and good health. Holy matrimony is also Your appointed means for bringing children into this world when it is Your will, and for nurturing them in the one true saving Christian faith.

On this our anniversary day, we give You thanks that You have brought us to this time of celebration. During our life together You have accompanied us with Your constant mercy and loving-kindness. In sorrow and sickness You have strengthened us. From temptation to infidelity and divorce You have delivered us. As You have forgiven all our sins because of the merits of our crucified and risen Lord Jesus Christ, You have enabled us to forgive one another. Through fidelity and perseverance we have sought to honor the perfect fidelity of Your Son, who strayed not from His ordained path, but was faithful unto death, even death on a cross. Trusting in His grace alone, we implore You to preserve us in faith and grant us continuing wedded bliss until this life's end and our Lord Jesus comes again to usher all believers into the celestial wedding hall for the celebration that has no end. In His name we pray. Amen. (122)

AN EXPECTANT MOTHER'S PRAYER

O great God and Father of all who call upon You, magnificent are Your works; I glorify Your holy name. You are my helper; complete what You have begun in me, and keep this child safe from all harm, and daily bestow on us health and strength. Guide me through Your Spirit, and let me be constantly mindful of my privilege and my responsibility as a mother. At all times let me place my trust in You and Your fatherly care, knowing that from generation to generation Your mercy is upon those who lean upon You. I commit both my child and myself to Your mercy and goodness. Relying on Jesus, my dear Redeemer, I pray, give me calmness, patience, and quiet happiness, and make me, in good time, a joyous mother of a happy child; in Jesus' name. Amen. (123)

FATHER'S THANKSGIVING AFTER CHILDBIRTH

O God, Creator of life, You have again revealed Yourself in the beautiful miracle of birth; thank You for alleviating my wife's pain and for holding Your protecting hand over her during delivery. Thank You for Your mercy; it was Your power that preserved her, Your goodness that delivered her, Your hand that supported us both.

You have lent us this precious child for our comfort and joy; give us grace to cherish him (her). Take us and this child into Your tender mercy, and keep us always safe with You. Defend him (her) from all dangers of body and soul, delivering him (her) safely to the waters of his (her) Baptism, where he (she) will receive the righteousness of Your Son, Jesus, and become Your beloved child; through Jesus Christ. Amen. (124)

AT THE BIRTH OF A CHILD

With joy and thanksgiving we praise You out of the fullness of our grateful hearts that You have gladdened our home and life with this newborn babe.

We know that this child is a gift of Your bountiful hand. Grant us grace and wisdom to bring up this precious soul in the knowledge and understanding of Your Word, which makes us wise unto salvation. Watch over him (her) with Your tenderest care and continued grace until the day we bring this little one to the font of Holy Baptism.

As surely as You will endow our child with faith and strengthen him (her) in spirit, so too endow our child with a healthy body, and strengthen and preserve him (her) according to Your good and gracious will. Grant that our child may grow in favor with You and bring sunshine and joy into our hearts and our home.

Keep us all in Your grace, forgiving us daily our sins and filling our souls with peace. You are our hiding place. And now to You be praise, glory, and thanksgiving, for this precious gift, this day and forever; through Jesus Christ, who is the Friend of children and the Savior of all. Amen. (125)

AT THE BAPTISM OF A CHILD

Heavenly Father, You once judged the wicked world with a flood but saved and preserved Noah and his family in the ark. You once drowned Pharaoh and his army but delivered Your people Israel and led them through the Red Sea. When Your Son, Jesus Christ, was baptized, You set apart the Jordan River and all water to be a flood that washes away all sins. Now look with favor upon (*name*), that, through Your Holy Spirit, he (she) may be blessed with true faith. Use this saving flood of Baptism to wash away the sin that he (she) has inherited from Adam, and separate him (her) from the number of unbelievers. Preserve him (her) dry and secure in the holy ark of Your Christian Church, and make him (her) fervent in spirit and joyful in hope as he (she) walks through the wilderness of this life trusting in Your flood of forgiveness. Make (*name*) worthy to attain eternal life and keep him (her) watchful for Your Son's return, when He will bring all believers to His eternal promised land. In Your holy name I pray. Amen. (126)

OF A SPONSOR

Dear Lord Jesus, I thank You for the honor of being a sponsor for (*name*). You have brought (*name*) into Your kingdom through the washing of water and Your Word, and You have forgiven all his (her) sins. Since Your Holy Spirit has given (*name*) faith in You for life and salvation, help me to be a good example of Christian faith and life for him (her), so that he (she) may learn to observe everything that You have commanded. Help (*name*) to learn from Your Word of truth that You love him (her) with an everlasting love. Help him (her) to learn the Ten Commandments, the Apostles' Creed, and the Lord's Prayer. Help him (her) to attend the services of Your house, hear Your life-giving Word, and learn to sing Your praises. Please keep (*name*) faithful to You and bring him (her) one day to Your Table, where You will strengthen his (her) faith as he (she) eats and drinks Your own body and blood in Holy Communion. Please keep (*name*) faithful to You and Your Church throughout his (her) life, and finally bring him (her) to Your eternal wedding feast. In Your holy name I pray. Amen. (127)

OF PARENTS

Lord Jesus, when parents brought their children to You so that You could touch them and bless them, You said, "Let the little children come to Me" (Matthew 19:14). I thank You for giving (*name*) to me to raise according to Your Word and for bringing him (her) to Yourself through the waters of Holy Baptism. Thank You for forgiving all of his (her) sins, for rescuing him (her) from death and the devil, and for giving him (her) eternal life as You promise in Your Word. I thank You for touching my son (daughter) through the washing of water and Your Word. Please bless me, and give me wisdom to teach (*name*) Your Word of truth and life, and help him (her) to learn the joys of Your forgiveness. Help him (her) to learn the Ten Commandments, the Apostles' Creed, and the Lord's Prayer. When I bring (*name*) to Your house, help him (her) to learn how much You love him (her), and help (*name*) to love and worship You, Your heavenly Father, and the Holy Spirit. Please strengthen the faith of (*name*), and bring him (her) one day to Your Table, where he (she) will eat and drink Your body and blood in Communion and receive Your forgiveness, life, and salvation. Amen. (128)

OF CHILDREN

Lord Jesus, who bid that even little children should be brought that You could bless them, bless me also, a child of the heavenly Father redeemed by Your gracious mercy and all sufficient suffering and death. Keep me faithful, steadfast, and loyal to You. Teach me to do Your will and follow graciously Your Word. Lord Jesus, grant me strength to do those things that become a child of God. Give me grace that I may be obedient to the instruction of my parents.

Bless Father and Mother; preserve them for many years to come. I thank You that You have given me parents who provide for the needs of body and soul. Make me appreciative of the Christian home and training I am receiving. May I find joy in the reading and studying of Your Word and grow steadily in the knowledge of Your saving Gospel.

Protect us as we go in and out of this house, that we may be gathered home safely each day. I ask all this in Jesus' name. Amen. (129)

LUTHER'S TABLE PRAYER— ASKING A BLESSING*

The eyes of all look to You, [O Lord,] and You give them their food at the proper time. You open Your hand and satisfy the desires of every living thing. (Psalm 145:15–16)

Lord God, heavenly Father, bless us and these Your gifts which we receive from Your bountiful goodness, through Jesus Christ, our Lord. Amen. (130)

LUTHER'S TABLE PRAYER— RETURNING THANKS*

Give thanks to the LORD, for He is good. His love endures forever. [He] gives food to every creature. He provides food for the cattle and for the young ravens when they call. His pleasure is not in the strength of the horse, nor His delight in the legs of a man; the Lord delights in those who fear Him, who put their hope in His unfailing love. (Psalm 136:1, 25; 147:9–11)

We thank You, Lord God, heavenly Father, for all Your benefits, through Jesus Christ, our Lord, who lives and reigns with You and the Holy Spirit forever and ever. Amen. (131)

*From Luther's Small Catechism.

FOR AN ERRING CHILD

Lord Jesus, You came into the world to seek and to save those who were separated from Your love. It is with a heavy and aching heart that I come to You, the Savior of sinners, imploring You to restore to saving faith my erring child. O Lord, my heart is breaking as I realize that my son (daughter) is following the way of unrepentant sinners, which always leads to condemnation. Save him (her), O Lord, save him (her). You have, in Your vast mercy performed many wonders, and I pray that You would lead back all the erring lambs who have wandered away from Your fold.

O Lord, if by any fault or neglect of my own I have caused him (her) to have strayed from You, I beg of Your mercy that You would forgive me. Guide me by Your Holy Word, and show me how to share Your love, mercy, and forgiveness. Draw all of us closer to

You in faith. If it be Your will, let this erring child be returned so that our hearts are filled again with Your peace and Your joy. Unite us with You in faith, and abide in our hearts both now and forevermore as our loving, compassionate, and forgiving Savior. In Your holy name I pray. Amen. (132)

FOR ONE WHO HAS STRAYED FROM THE FAITH

Lord Jesus Christ, You are the friend of sinners, the shepherd who seeks the lost sheep. I come to You, Lord, in humble repentance, as one who was lost and dead in sin. Yet, by Your grace I was baptized into the name of the triune God and made an heir of everlasting life.

You have blessed me with the nourishment of Word and Sacrament, where I receive constant forgiveness and the power of the Spirit to renew my life. As You have gifted me, O Lord, so work Your salvation for (*name*), who at this time seems far away from Your cross and the Word of God.

Lord, You know all things; You know how Satan works to deceive, how he would lead even the elect away if he could. He uses our selfish natures to make us believe that it is okay to do things our way, to trust our own judgment, to ignore Your commands. Bring (*name*) to the judgment of Your Law, so that he (she) may see the condemnation of sin and his (her) alienation from God. Bless him (her) with the forgiving Word of Gospel that he (she) might believe in You, O Christ, and have the joy of forgiveness and the living hope of eternal life.

Help me, Lord, to be an instrument in Your hands to regain this lost soul; in Jesus' name. Amen. (133)

STRIFE IN THE HOME

Father of all, who blesses us beyond measure, You placed us together that we might be a help to each other, that we would support and strengthen the other, not only for the trials of this life, but also in faith and for the life to come. Have mercy on us; I have not lived my life according to Your will, and by choosing my will over Yours, I have brought strife into my home.

O God, You know how prone my heart is to mistrust, temper, lack of patience, and strife. Forgive me for praying so little, for my want of love, for stubbornly insisting on my rights and my own way. Come to us and help us. Make us to know again that without Your peace our hearts will have no peace. Give us, O God, the will and the means to be reconciled to You and to one another; join us to Yourself through Word and Sacrament, that we may live together and with You in the peace that only You can give; through Your Son, our Lord Jesus Christ. Amen. (134)

ON OCCUPYING A NEW HOME

O Lord, as I (we) enter into my (our) new home, come with me (us), and let Your divine presence bless me (us) with the riches of Your grace. Guard my (our) entering and leaving. Grant that I (we) may keep out of this home all selfishness, pride, and thoughtlessness. Let Your Word abide among all who enter here, that knowing first Your love-bought peace, I (we) may love and be at peace with my (our) neighbors, and that by my (our) living, I (we) may bring glory and honor to You as the master of this household and the defender of this home; through Jesus Christ our Lord. Amen. (135)

FOR THE HOME

Lord God, our home is among the most precious gifts we receive in this life. We realize this all the more as we remember our Lord Jesus. He set aside home and family. Having no place to lay His head throughout His ministry, He chose to sojourn among those He came to save. We prayerfully invite Him to dwell in our earthly abode even as He continually invites us by Word and Sacrament to dwell forever in our heavenly home, which He prepares for us.

Make us ever grateful for this shelter from life's storms. Keep this house always the home of comfort, joy, peace, and forgiveness. According to Your will, protect us not only from the spiritual assaults of Satan, but likewise make our home a fortress against the calamities of nature and the wickedness of sinful man.

Grant us the virtue of hospitality, the joy of harmonious living, and the blessing of gathering around Your Word and bringing our family's prayers before You. May all who dwell in our home be blessed by Your presence and Your peace, and may all who go forth give thanks for the grace they receive from You through us, Your dear children. We receive Your loving-kindness in our home as a reminder of the eternal home we inherit through Your Son, Jesus Christ, in whose name we pray. Amen. (136)

FOR THOSE AWAY FROM HOME

Lord, gracious and merciful, who watches over even the sparrow and upholds everything with Your everlasting arms, protect and keep my loved ones while they are away from home. Watch over them tenderly so that no evil comes to them during our separation. Keep them faithful to Your Word and Your Church. Guard and protect them as they are tempted by the lusts of sin and the unbelief of the world.

Keep them pure in heart, clean in mind, and healthy in body. Dwell in them day by day. Abide with those of us left behind as well as those who go, and bring them safely home to me and at last to the eternal home in heaven. To You both now and forever be glory and praise, world without end; through Jesus Christ, our Lord. Amen. (137)

WHILE AWAY FROM HOME

O Lord, who is present everywhere, be very near to those at home, and protect them from every danger of body and soul.

Heavenly Father, You comfort me and all Your children with the promises of Your Word that You are our hiding place and refuge—a very present help in every situation of life. As the caretaker of all who call on You, grant that these promises may give me needed spiritual security. Gracious Lord, turn all things to the good of those who love You, and therefore direct all things in our lives and homes to our eternal welfare.

Increase my love for You. You came to me in Baptism, that by grace I might be Your child and You my loving Father. Strengthen me in this gracious gift, that I might ever stand in the blessings bestowed through water and the Word. I confess that I have not always loved You with all my heart, yet in mercy You do not turn away from me. O compassionate Lord, forgive me all my sin. Protect all whom I love during the coming night. Unite us together with You through Your Word and holy Sacrament, through our faith and eternal hope, and in our common confession of our one Lord, until that time when You bring me safely home. In Jesus' name I ask this. Amen. (138)

FOR A MEMBER OF THE FAMILY IN DANGER

O God, You are my rock, my fortress, my deliverer. Imploring Your mercy, I come to You in this hour of great danger and distress for a family member. I put all my trust in You. Help me remain calm, composed, confident, and trustful, for You are with me. In You alone I find comfort and strength. Forgive my anxiety and my little faith. Keep me from doubting that You are in control. Even in these distressing moments, I give You all honor, glory, and praise, for in You alone do I put my trust.

Your will be done, O Lord. May it be a gracious and compassionate will. Today I look through a glass darkly, but in You there is no darkness. Grant me strength to believe that You work all things together for good for those who love You.

Good and gracious God, uphold my loved one during this time of tremendous trial. Grant strength of faith, courage, perseverance, and Your peace, which surpasses all understanding. Please protect my family member who is danger, and above all, preserve us in Your grace now and forever, through my Lord and Savior, Jesus Christ. Amen. (139)

A SOLDIER'S PRAYER

Dear Father in heaven, I ask for Your protection and guidance as I serve my country. By the blood of Your Son You have bought me, and You have made me Your own dear child by Holy Baptism. In Your Word You have given me the assurance that the very hairs of my head are numbered. Trusting in Your promise and relying upon Your grace, I confidently ask You to protect me against all danger and deliver me from every evil of body and soul. O Jesus, my Redeemer, let me never forget at what cost You have redeemed me. May the word of Your bitter suffering and death ever bring me repentance unto forgiveness. Keep me from sin and wickedness, indifference to Your mercy, and coldness of heart. Keep me mindful of Your gift of Baptism by which You have cleansed me from all my sins, and renew me to follow in Your way and do Your will by Your grace. O Holy Spirit, strengthen me in the hour of temptation. Keep me pure in heart and chaste in body, obedient to my superiors, and considerate of all those who serve with me, that I might give witness to the Christian faith into which You have called me. O God of my salvation, let me be and remain Yours now and forever for Jesus' sake. Amen. (140)

A SAILOR'S PRAYER

Gracious Father, Your Spirit moved over the face of the waters as You, by Your Word—my Lord Jesus Christ—called light out of darkness. Thank You that the same Holy Spirit was present with Your Word in the waters of my Baptism. You brought me out of the darkness of sin into Your light. Often, out here at sea, I feel loneliness descending on me like a cloud. Father, remind me that You are always with me. In these times, far from home, preserve and strengthen me in the faith, so that I may always know Your fatherly love. May the water that surrounds me remind me of my Baptism. Lord, I often hunger for the comfort of Christ's bodily presence in the Sacrament of the Altar.

Grant that I may soon receive it from the hand of one of Your faithful ministers.

Precious Jesus, You know life at sea, going to sea with Your disciples and comforting them in the storm. In dangerous storms, hold Your guarding hand over our ship. Knowing Your peace, may neither my shipmates nor I give in to fear and despair. You are mightier than many waters! Grant me, therefore, Your peace and see me safely to shore, that in the end I enter the safe harbor of Your eternal presence to live with You forever. Amen. (141)

AN AVIATOR'S PRAYER

Eternal Lord, who commands the winds to cease with a word and protects the eagle in its flight and the dove seeking shelter, uphold me as I soar into the sky and fly above land and sea. Pilot my ship safely through the air, and give me nerves that are steady and relaxed, a mind calm and composed, as I fly on to my destination. Give me a successful takeoff and at journey's end a safe landing, that no harm come to me and those entrusted to my care.

Hold Your protecting hand over me as I pass through cloud and storm, and let me not lose my way as I fly by instrument through the darkness. Above all, keep me in Your grace and favor for Jesus' sake, and let my last landing bring me safely into Your presence, redeemed and saved to praise You forever. Amen. (142)

A PUBLIC SAFETY OFFICER'S PRAYER

O God of order and Lord of all power, You have established law and order so that we might live quiet, peaceable, and godly lives in this brief earthly pilgrimage. I thank and praise You that in my vocation as a police/fire/emergency medical officer, You have allowed me a part in Your work of preserving the life and property You have graciously given Your children on earth. You know, dear Father, that my work is fraught with danger and sorrow, frustration and temptation, and I acknowledge that I cannot succeed in it without Your constant care. When I am weak, give me strength; when afraid, courage; when tempted to do wrong, Your Holy Spirit; when unappreciated, the assurance of Your own approval; and when I have sinned, the certainty that all my transgressions have been fully atoned for by Christ, my loving Lord. Comfort, I pray, my loved ones, who share the joys and sorrows of my vocation with me. Bless my fellow officers and the people we serve, for into Your hands I commend myself, my body and soul, and all things. Amen. (143)

FOR FAITHFUL WORK

Almighty God and Father, without whose help and blessing all labor is in vain, remember me in my work this day. If it be Your will, give me a prosperous day and lead me to find satisfaction and contentment in the tasks at hand. May all my work be done well, that I may glorify You with honest work; for the sake of Him who completed His work for us, even Jesus Christ our Lord. Amen. (144)

FOR JOY IN MY JOB

Heavenly Father, Creator of heaven and earth, it is out of Your love and wisdom that You gave me work to do and fitted me in body and mind to do this work. And yet my sinful will too often dreads the workday and casts about for other things to do. But You, O God, have called me to this work. Forgive me my sin. Strengthen me by Your Spirit that I may see that my place of work is a field of Your service to my family, my fellow worker, and my neighbor. Give me joy in my vocation, and make me glad and grateful for the strength to serve You; through Jesus Christ. Amen. (145)

FOR COMFORT CONCERNING VOCATION

Dear Lord, I have Your Word, and I trust that You certainly bless me in my present calling—this I know. Yet I look around and see everywhere a lack of answers, a lack of help, and a lack of that which I need now! I can turn to no one for help except to You. Help me with all of this. My comfort is in this: You have said and commanded that I should ask, search, and knock, and so doing I will certainly receive, find, and have that which I desire. Amen. (146)

OF ONE WHO IS IN BUSINESS

Lord, You have prospered the labor of my hands and have given success to my undertakings. Oh, kind and gracious Father, grant me always a grateful heart, that I may never forget how completely unworthy I am of all the mercies and of all the truth You have shown Your servant. Grant me a lively sense of my responsibilities and obligations, which You have placed upon me. Deeply impress upon me the need of remaining humble, of trusting not in wealth or material goods but in You, the living God, and in Your Son, my only Savior. Keep me mindful that You, who have so richly given me all things to enjoy, can quickly take away all that I have. Teach me, O God of love, to be rich in good works, always ready to help my brothers and sisters, ever willing to contribute, according to my ability, toward the building up of Your kingdom, both here and abroad. By the power of Your Spirit, help me to store up treasure not merely upon this earth, but especially in heaven, which Christ has procured for me by the payment of His precious blood. Amen. (147)

IN BUSINESS REVERSALS

The Lord gave, and the Lord has taken away; blessed be the name of the Lord! My dear heavenly Father, Your poor, tormented child flees to You for comfort, peace of mind, guidance, and help. You know better than I the worries and anxious feelings troubling my heart and my mind. There is nowhere else to go in my distress but to You, my gracious Father.

Humble me under Your mighty hand, so that I may cast all my cares upon You, the One who loves and cares for me. I know that even these business reversals are sent as a needed humbling for my eternal welfare. Heavenly Father, for the sake of Your Son, my Redeemer, forgive me all my sins. May these losses teach me to know the uncertainty and vanity of all earthly possessions. Create in me that godliness and contentment that is of greater gain.

According to Your gracious and holy will, lead me to success and prosperity. If not, then, Lord, let me become richer in faith and in good works. Supply me each day with daily bread, and grant me the grace to live trustingly and to remain as Your loving, obedient child, even as You correct me. Enable me to firmly cling to the words of Your promise: "I will never leave you nor forsake you" (Hebrews 13:5). Your will be done, my heavenly Father; for Jesus' sake. Amen. (148)

LUTHER'S PRAYER BASED ON "CAST ALL YOUR CARES UPON GOD, FOR HE CARES FOR YOU"*

Heavenly Father, You are indeed my Lord and God, who has created me when I was but nothing. In addition, You have saved me through Your Son. Now You have appointed me to this official responsibility and set this work before me. It does not proceed according to my will, and it is so great that it would otherwise weigh heavily on me and cause me great fear, that I of my own ability could find neither counsel nor help. Therefore, let everything be commended unto You, give me counsel and help, and remain faithful in everything, as You have promised. Amen. (149)

*See 1 Peter 5:7.

DURING HARD TIMES

Lord, have mercy. Christ, have mercy. Lord, have mercy. Merciful Father, You know how difficult these days are for me. In Your holy Word You have promised to hear those who cry unto You in the day of trouble. Listen to my cries for mercy and send me help from the sanctuary of Your grace. Preserve me from bitterness of spirit, and rescue me from every temptation to despair. Calm my frustrations with the knowledge that my life is secure in Your redeeming love, for I am baptized into the death and resurrection of Your Son. Draw me out of self-centered worry, which stifles faith, and cause me to take comfort in the great and precious promises that You have made to me and all believers in the Gospel. Sustain and strengthen me under every cross and affliction, that Your grace might be made perfect in my weakness. Give me confidence to pray without losing heart and to trust in Your mighty deliverance according to Your good and gracious will. Father, into Your hands I commend myself. Hear me, for the sake of Your Son, who alone is my Brother and Savior. Amen. (150)

OF A FAMILY DURING UNEMPLOYMENT

Heavenly Father, we come to You for aid and encouragement during these days of unemployment. Give us a fuller measure of faith in the promises of Your Word. Grant that we may live trustingly one day at a time, knowing that You will not fail us. Even the little we receive we accept with grateful hearts. Protect us from the dangers of enforced idleness, unnecessary worry, and sleepless nights. Provide for our family, and supply the means to find regular employment. Root out greed, selfishness, and all other distress in our family. Grant us success, earnestness, sobriety, and skill as we seek work. Heavenly Father, You bless a person through the labor of his hands, satisfy our hunger with bread, and comfort our souls with the peace that comes only from our relationship with You; through Jesus, our Lord. Amen. (151)

AT TIMES OF PERSONAL UNEMPLOYMENT

O God, You have been my help in past days, and in the same way I ask You not to turn away from me in this present day as I walk the streets, discouraged and disheartened, seeking work. Lead me and direct me to find suitable work.

O Lord, my sins are ever before me. In my yesterdays I have not always served You; too often I have ignored Your goodness and Your mercy. Forgive me, and let me find peace for my soul in You. Take all resentment, bitterness, and rebellion out of my heart and spirit. Make me hopeful, cheerful, courageous, patient, and confident.

You have promised to be with me in the day of trouble. Open Your hands and satisfy my needs. Teach me to face the day confident of Your goodness. O Lord, let me not doubt Your promises. Hear the cry of my distressed heart and disturbed mind. Have mercy upon me; for Jesus' sake. Amen. (152)

THANKSGIVING FOR GOD'S BLESSING AND CARE

Lord Jesus, I come to You today to give thanks for all of Your blessings and for Your care. I know that I have deserved none of Your gifts, for I am a sinner who never stops sinning. Day by day I have burdened You with my selfishness, my disregard for Your Law, and my callous attitude concerning Your cross, which was borne for me. Yet, in spite of what I am, You have blessed me with forgiveness, life, and salvation. You grant me the gifts of Word and Sacrament, wherein I can find my sins exposed but also the great grace that covers them all.

Beyond these greatest of gifts, You have blessed me with earthly life, in which the Holy Spirit worked faith in You. In this earthly life, I have received Your gifts of sustenance, of job and home, of family and friends, and of fellow worshipers of Your name. You have provided job and resources, health and healing, and the wherewithal to live and move and have my being. You have given me life here and life beyond. The magnitude of Your grace and mercy is beyond my comprehension. I live in awe of You! Accept my humble thanks this day for Your blessings and care; in Your name. Amen. (153)

AT TIMES OF ILLNESS IN THE FAMILY

Almighty God, with whom all things are possible, hear our prayer as we come to You in trouble and distress. You are our hiding place. You are our very present help in trouble. We have no other refuge in an hour like this. Gracious Lord, You can heal. Your grace can restore to health and give us strength to carry on. We know that You are compassionate, for You have sent Your beloved Son, Jesus Christ, to suffer the death of the cross in order to redeem us and make us Your own. As You did not forsake Him, surely You will not abandon us in this time of great need. As You raised Him from the dead on the third day, so we ask that You would also raise us up with Him from this present danger. O Lord, we humble ourselves before You and confess our many sins. We pray, merciful Father, for Your grace hour by hour. Forgive us and restore us, for You have made us Your own children in Christ. Remove the worries and anxious fears that would crush us. Give us grace to trust in You, whose will is wiser than our own, for we have been baptized into the death, burial, and resurrection of Christ Jesus, our Lord. Amen. (154)

AT THE APPROACH OF DEATH

O Lord, one whom I love and care about is dying. Yet Your love of him (her) is still greater, for You have redeemed him (her) with the precious blood of Your Son. If it be Your will that he (she) should pass out of this mortal life, receive him (her) to Yourself in glory. If this be his (her) last night on earth, let Your holy angels take him (her) into Your presence, where there is no more pain and suffering and sin, but fullness of joy forevermore. Wash him (her) of all sin, and accept him (her) for Jesus' sake. Strengthen our faith, and keep us close to You. In Jesus' name we ask it. Amen. (155)

AFTER A DEATH

Amid my tears, O Lord, I praise You that You have received (*name*) to Yourself in glory for all eternity. I thank You that You have brought him (her) to the knowledge of Jesus Christ, our Lord and Savior. Comfort all who mourn with the glorious hope of the resurrection and life eternal. Grant me grace to say with a believing heart, "Thy will be done," and to know that Your will is a good and gracious will, even in the present hour. Comfort me through Your Gospel, which promises strength and help to the troubled and weary. O Lord, forsake me not in this hour. Prepare me through Your Word and Sacrament for that day when You will call me to Yourself, that I may joyfully join the whole company of heaven to live with You forever; for Jesus' sake I ask it. Amen. (156)

OF A WIDOW

Blessed Lord and beloved Savior, comfort me, Your poor handmaiden, especially in this time of grief and sorrow and such terrible bereavement. You have given me an image of Yourself in the person of my dear husband, whom You have now taken from me to Yourself in heaven. Oh, how my feelings overwhelm me, and I am so alone! Lord, help me! You are the One who brought me to my husband and united me to him as one flesh. Under You alone, he was my head, my protector, my companion in this world, my friend, and my greatest earthly joy. Indeed, my entire life—my body, mind, and spirit—has been intertwined with his. Now that death has parted us, who shall be my helper? I am overcome, and very nearly undone, with loneliness and fear, with mourning, and with anxiety for the future.

Dear Lord Jesus, I do not desire to mourn like those who have no hope. Your Word and Spirit teach me that my help, at all times, comes from You. Forgive me for my misplaced trust in the strength and glory of man. Cleanse me of my sinful worries and concerns when I sink into doubt, as though You had not conquered death and risen from the dead. Lord, I do believe, but I need You every day and night to help my unbelief. Give me the faith and confidence to seek You where You may be found, within Your holy Church, in the preaching of Your sweet Gospel, and in the Supper of Your true body and true blood. Bring me joyfully and often to that great banquet of Your kingdom, which has no end. In sure and certain hope, give me strength to face the long and difficult days ahead. Enable me to make wise decisions and to deal with so many new responsibilities. Bless my efforts and correct all my errors. And as I entrust my days and burdens to Your care, grant to me each night a peaceful and quiet sleep, until I shall also fall asleep in You and live forever in Your presence. Amen. (157)

OF A WIDOWER

Father of mercy and God of all comfort, my only help in all my need, You give and take away according to Your wisdom. You bring down the proud and raise up those whom You have humbled. I cry to You now out of the depths of my sadness, with groans of misery too deep for words, because, through temporal death, You have taken from my side the dear woman whom You gave to be with me. My loss is great, for she has been the delight of my eyes, my true companion, the glory of my house, the one in whom my heart could safely trust regarding all that concerns my earthly welfare.

Lord, look upon my tears, consider my agony of heart and mind and soul, and forgive me all my sin. Do not leave me in despair. You have said, "It is not good that the man should be alone" (Genesis 2:18), yet I am now bereft of my helpmate; I am alone and miserable. Comfort me with Your gracious presence, for the fear in my heart is great. Therefore, teach me by Your Spirit through Word and Sacrament that You are with me and have not left me without consolation.

I confess that, as a husband, I have been a poor reflection of that dear Savior, Jesus Christ. But do not allow my failings to give the devil any foothold in my life. I pray to You in all humility, in repentance and with faith in Your forgiveness: prevent me from becoming lost in my misery. Nor let me falter, in my grief, in those other vocations and responsibilities that remain to me. Enable me to serve my family and neighbor faithfully, even as You continue to serve and protect me. Into Your hands, O Lord, I commend myself entirely; let me never come to ruin. Be my comfort, my shield and strength, my fortress and strong tower, my help and constant companion, that I may praise You for Your faithfulness unto all eternity; through Christ, my Lord. Amen. (158)

OF ONE WHO IS SINGLE

Merciful Father, You have promised to sustain us, Your children, throughout our earthly pilgrimage, whatever it may be that You have planned. St. Paul, as a single person, lived out his entire earthly pilgrimage willingly, with graciousness and thanksgiving. I fervently pray that You will sustain me with the same spirit. Grant me the willingness to accept my vocation as a single person, and grant me sustenance through the body of Christ. Continue to surround me with family and friends, and grant me the opportunity to serve You and Your Church. Finally, grant me the ability to live out my earthly pilgrimage with contentment and joy. Amen. (159)

OF AN ELDERLY PERSON (1)

Lord God, our continual refuge, our life in old age, in whose hands our time abides, look! The years that do not please me have come upon me. For my abilities in this advanced age are continually being taken from me, and all about me, difficulties and weaknesses have increased in number. You have so graciously and fatherly cared for me from the time that I was in the womb. Until now, from my youth, You have remained my hope. Therefore, I humbly ask You not to depart from me in my old age, in which I have grown gray and weak, but until my life's blessed end lift me up, bear me, and save me. Especially I pray to You, O gracious Father, that You would govern and lead me with Your Holy Spirit, that I may wholly dedicate the rest of my time on earth to be with You, so that, even in my sighing, I may remain faithful on this Christian pilgrimage. Strengthen me in this time of preparation for a blessed end. May I be ready, so that if today or tomorrow my life should reach its goal, I may, with old Simeon, in peace depart this world unto life eternal. Amen. (160)

OF AN ELDERLY PERSON (2)

O Lord Jesus Christ, my own Savior, who does not spurn the sighs of the miserable or despise the longing of grieving hearts, to You I cry from the depths of great sorrow that in these later years of my life I find myself alone. I feel so alone and miserable that I have become estranged from my friends and relatives. My friends have forgotten me, and my neighbors have drawn themselves away from me. To You I humbly pray, that in grace You would look upon my misery and stand by me, not like the world that so exalts in the strength and vigor of youth and leaves the old to their loneliness, but according to Your sure promise. Lord, were I to have You alone, I would have no need to desire anything else in heaven or on earth. And were all the world to forget me, yet You remain my heart's only comfort, then I have a certain and faithful friend in life and death. My hope is placed in You, O Lord; leave me in ruin nevermore! Amen. (161)

OF ONE IN LOVE

O Lord, who directs our lives day after day, I thank You that You have so graciously led me through the days of my youth and have preserved me from straying and falling. I come to You for special guidance in these days when I am choosing a life companion. Lord, look down the pathway of my life, and if this woman (man) is truly a fitting partner and companion for me, then grant that our lives may be fused into one and that we may journey on together happily.

Keep me pure in heart. Grant that I may do nothing against Your commandments and offend You. Grant that my conduct may faithfully reflect that I am a child of God.

O Lord, if it be Your will, grant that we may understand each other better from day to day and love each other sincerely. Above all, give us the grace to keep You in our hearts as our friend and guide. I ask this for the sake of Jesus, my Lord and Savior. Amen. (162)

FOR A PIOUS SPOUSE

O almighty and eternal God, Creator, Preserver, and Multiplier of the human race, You instituted marriage while Adam and Eve still dwelt in paradise. You also honored holy matrimony by the first miracle performed by Your dear Son, Jesus Christ, our Savior, at the wedding in Cana of Galilee. You know my heart, You know my disposition and attributes, and You know my weaknesses and strengths better than I myself. From You one also receives the gift of a good spouse because that comes alone from the Most High. I beseech You from the heart that You would grant me a good, Christian, God-fearing spouse whom I would ever hold dear in my heart. I pray that this companion and I might peacefully and harmoniously live upon earth in the true fear of God and in this Christian journey. I cry to You, make my heart fit regarding such things, and enlighten me with Your Holy Spirit. And having commended the matter to Your fatherly care, let me be at peace; for the sake of Jesus Christ. Amen. (163)

OF THOSE ENGAGED UPON THEIR ENGAGEMENT

O gracious, bounteous, and merciful God, Father of our Lord Jesus Christ and Creator of heaven and earth, You have instituted and ordered the holy estate of marriage in Your divine wisdom, ordaining that man and wife should dwell together in honorable fellowship. We offer You heartfelt praise and thanks that You have brought us to the point that we wish for nothing greater than the day in which this engagement might be confirmed in full through the proper, public joining in matrimony by the hand of the pastor. We therefore ask You in all humility to preserve each of us in good health until the appointed day, that we may joyfully experience our marriage day and our public entry into the church as a married couple. Grant us grace and blessing in the meantime, so that we might contemplate our future together as man and wife. Give us the will and strength to honor Your commandment concerning marriage, that we may approach Your altar in purity. May we ever give You honor and praise through our Lord Jesus Christ, who lives and reigns with You and the Holy Spirit, one God, now and forever. Amen. (164)

OF A COUPLE ON THEIR WEDDING DAY

Almighty God, heavenly Father, who instituted, ordered, and blessed the estate of marriage, we give You praise and thanks that You have also called us to this estate and have protected us from scandal up to this time. Since we know that the devil is a great enemy of this, Your ordinance of marriage, we therefore ask You today that You would array about us Your holy angels, that they would protect and defend us from the devil's murderousness and lies in this our estate. May You also guide and govern us by Your Holy Spirit, that we might love Your divine commandments above all things and serve You with a true heart. May it thus be that we, as spouses, being each a part of the other, might display marital faithfulness, love, honor, and blessing. May we live long together with each other according to our promised marriage vows in health, peace, rest, and unity. May we bring forth children according to Your divine will. May every other matter that we may take up or refrain from doing be alone to Your divine praise and honor, to the end that we, after this life is past, might also possess eternal life in each other's company. Amen. (165)

Personal Prayers of the Sick, the Convalescing, and the Dying

OF ONE WHO IS ILL (1)

Lord, with my anxious cares and troubles I come to You, trusting in Your Word and believing in Your promises. You know that I have been greatly upset by the worries, fears, and doubts of the day. You must be my strength and refuge if I am to find peace of mind and healing for my body. Uphold me with Your almighty arm.

I am not worthy of Your love and mercy, for I have sinned and often done evil in Your sight. Blot out all my transgressions through Christ's precious blood. Fill my soul with peace. Give me the grace to put all my trust in You. Let Your healing hand rest upon me day after day. Enable me by Your grace to rise above all my suffering to praise You, whose will is wiser than my own. Keep my household and me in Your saving grace, and abide with us all the days of our lives; through Jesus Christ, our Lord. Amen. (166)

OF ONE WHO IS ILL (2)

Lord Jesus, strength of the weary and a very present help to all who are in distress, I come to You with my many burdens and sins. Cleanse my soul, O Lord, and heal my body. Safely see me through the troubled waters of the day. Remove all sinful thoughts and worries from my heart, and let me find peace in You. Lead me again to Calvary to behold Your boundless love, O gracious Savior. Fill my soul with the joy of forgiveness and the hope of everlasting life. Let not the sufferings and cares of this day make me despondent. Teach me to believe that Your abiding presence will uphold me from hour to hour. Give me peaceful days and restful nights. Bless me with a refreshing sleep. Come to me with healing in Your wings. Speak to my soul the comforting promises of Your Word, and keep me steadfast in the faith to the end. Bless this household, and keep all of us cheerful, hopeful, and confident. I ask this of You who has redeemed me with Your own blood. Amen. (167)

OF ONE WHO IS ILL (3)

Divine Lord, You have been gracious and merciful to me in Christ Jesus. Forgive me all my sins day after day. Accept my thanks for this Your goodness. Let me find my joy in You, the one who has brought to my heart salvation and peace.

In Your mercy look upon my distress and pain, and forgive me all my sins and all my worry. Ease my sufferings, and make me patient and cheerful in my affliction. Bless those who take care of me. Let them not become weary in this service that they must render to me. Keep me faithful to Your Word, and grant that I may continue in Your grace until life's journey ends and I behold You in the glory of eternity; through Jesus Christ, our Lord. Amen. (168)

OF ONE WHO IS ILL (4)

Jesus, my Savior and the Shepherd of my soul, embrace me with Your love, and protect me throughout this day. I need You, for I am wounded and bruised, sick at heart, and in trouble and distress. To You I come. Forgive me all my sins in Your mercy and love, and uphold me amid these trials and tribulations. Strengthen my faith. Take every doubt out of my heart, and lead me into Your Word, where You promise to be with me always in every situation of life. Calm my nerves. Put my mind at ease. Make me hopeful and patient. O Christ, have mercy upon me. O Christ, be with me now and forever. Amen. (169)

BEFORE SURGERY

Heavenly Father, in this hour of anxiety I pray for Your divine presence and aid. As the time of the operation draws near, I need a staff on which to lean. To whom shall I turn but to You, gracious Lord? You have created, redeemed, and sanctified me. I am Your baptized and beloved child in Christ. You will not forsake me as I cry to You for strength in my trouble and pain. I confess to You my unworthiness, my many weaknesses, and my transgressions. You mercifully forgive me for the sake of the sacrifice of Your dear Son, my precious Savior. Give wisdom and skill to the doctors and nurses, that all they do will bring about a speedy recovery in keeping with Your good, fatherly will. I commend myself into Your hands. While I slumber and sleep, watch over me. Take every fear out of my heart. Comfort me with the assurance of my salvation through the blood of Your Son, Jesus Christ, and grant me a faith that clings only to Him, who is the great and eternal cure for all sin, sickness, and death. Your name I praise, O Lord of life and death. Hear my prayer for the sake of Your dear Son. Amen. (170)

AFTER SURGERY

Bless the Lord, O my soul, and all that is in me, bless His holy name. O merciful Father in heaven, You have fulfilled Your promises to me and have been with me in my hour of anxiety and pain. When I was weak and helpless, You were my strength. I called upon You in the day of trouble, and You delivered me. Now I glorify You. You gave to the surgeon and medical team skilled hands that have brought me through this operation. You did not count my sins against me, but have graciously forgiven them for Christ's sake. O gracious Father, continue Your mercies and, if it be Your will, grant me a full and speedy recovery. Bless me with a restful day and refreshing sleep this night. As You watch over me in these coming days of recovery, grant me patience, and let my thoughts dwell on Your goodness. You are my Shepherd; I shall not want. O gracious Father, I cast all my cares upon You, for You care for me. Hear my prayer for the sake of Jesus Christ. Amen. (171)

OF A CONVALESCENT (1)

Dear heavenly Father, I come before You in the name of my Lord Jesus, the Great Physician of body, mind, and soul. Even as Your hand chastises me out of fatherly, divine goodness and mercy, You also give me patience to endure and strength to overcome. You touch me with healing through the hands of those You call into the medical professions. You remind me of Your undying love through the voice of the pastor You call to be my shepherd. You bring comfort and peace through the visitation of those You call to be my family, friends, and fellow redeemed.

Having now received the beginnings of health and healing, I ask that You would continue my convalescence according to Your will. Make me a joyful recipient of Your grace and a grateful vessel of Your goodness, that I might respond as Your dear child while You continue to bring others into my life to ease the burdens You have laid upon me. Grant me patience that I might live according to Your will, strength that I might love my neighbor as myself, and healing that I might continue to gather with my brothers and sisters before Your altar. Bless those You use to effect my health and healing, that they might continue to fulfill their vocations in service to You. Amen. (172)

OF A CONVALESCENT (2)

Lord Jesus, as my thoughts return to the days of my anguish and pain, I gratefully remember Your gracious presence and merciful aid during those days of illness. Give me the resolve to fulfill the vows and pledges that rose from my heart to Your throne of mercy while I lay on my bed of torment, grief, and suffering. Lord, let me not, because of my restored health, forget the promises made in the days of my tribulation and sorrow. Lord, You didn't forsake me in my misfortune, so let me not turn away from You, either in life or in death. In days of health, let Your Word and Your holy will be the joy of my heart. In days of sorrow, let me prove that I have learned well the lessons You taught me in these times of trial.

Lord, You have taught me that tribulation works patience; and patience, experience; and experience, hope; and hope makes me not ashamed, because of Your love and Your light shed upon me by the Holy Spirit. Teach me to always say, "Thy will be done," with full assurance that all things work together for good to me and that no creature, no man, no devil, can ever pluck me out of Your hands, O precious Savior. Amen. (173)

DURING PROLONGED RECOVERY

Surely, O Lord, You made me Yours through water and Word and keep me with Jesus Christ in the one true faith, while yet You also chasten me with a persistent affliction. It drains my will, tests my patience, and challenges my endurance. You have promised that You will not impose upon Your children more than we can endure, and I know the truth of this word. However, I remain weak and days of full health and renewed vigor seem far away. I know not if I am closer to the beginning or the end of this trial. In weakness and uncertainty, sins of doubt and despair tempt me. Forgive these and all my other iniquities of thought, word, and deed.

Remind me of Your grace, keeping my eyes fixed on Jesus, the Author and Finisher of my faith. Allow me to serve You by gratefully receiving the services of those You call to meet my needs. Bless my pastor as he brings me Word and Supper and prays with and for me. Enlighten my health-care providers as they apply the knowledge and wisdom You have given them. Provide friends and family who bring true comfort. Lead me through this wilderness of testing for the sake of Your Son, Jesus, who knows my pain and weakness through His own temptation and passion. Amen. (174)

OF ONE SUFFERING CHRONIC ILLNESS OR DEBILITATION

Dear heavenly Father, I know You are the God who loves me, yet my life is a struggle. I am plagued with disease and pain, disability and incapacity. I cannot do for myself and am but a burden to others.

I do not doubt that You care, for You sent me Jesus. You encourage me to ask and I shall receive. However, You never promised what I would receive. What I have received seems so far from what I would desire. Your Word says that if earthly fathers can give good gifts to their children, how much more will not the perfect heavenly Father give good gifts to His children.

Knowing these things does not make me trust them. Teach me, Lord, to believe Your Word. Remind me that my troubles are not from You. They are the curse of my sinful nature. But I know that You know that curse of sin, for Jesus bore it on the cross for me, that I might have victory over it. Help me to grasp the meaning, the joy, and the inheritance of bliss that is mine in that cross. Let me see the grace of my Baptism, wherein I was made a member of God's family receiving forgiveness, life, and salvation.

Help me to trust the promise of salvation and with it all Your other promises, especially Your promise "I will never leave you nor forsake you" (Hebrews 13:5). Let these things sustain me in my daily struggle; in Jesus' name. Amen. (175)

DEVOTION AT THE APPROACH OF DEATH

I'm dying. I see it in the helpless look in my doctor's eyes. I hear it in the concerned voices of friends and family. Some are calling and visiting more often now; some are staying away. Cards are propped up all over my room. "Get well soon," they say. I know that will be, but not before I die. I feel the chill of death in my bones and smell it on my breath. Thoughts of death cloud my mind, especially in the dark hours of the night. Sleep is shallow and restless, yet I seem to crave sleep more and more. I am weary and my body aches. My appetite is gone. Each day seems to bring new losses, greater weakness.

Have mercy on me, O Lord. I fear Your judgments, for they are just and true. "The wages of sin is death" (Romans 6:23), and my death is just and well deserved. I am a sinner, from the moment You breathed life into me until the day of my death; I am a child of Adam, doomed to die. My sin is always before me, now more than ever as I lie on my bed and ponder my life. O Father, how I have sinned against You and those around me! I am ashamed even to admit it.

I sometimes try to minimize it to others and say, "I've lived a good life," but I know the truth. Every day of my life has been soiled with sin. I am afraid of dying. I fear the unknown; I fear losing hold on my life.

And yet, by Your grace, I am unafraid. Your psalmist says, "Precious in the sight of the LORD is the death of His saints" (Psalm 116:15), and the Holy Spirit cries out from heaven, "Blessed are [those] who die in the Lord" (Revelation 14:13). I cling to these words. Your Son, Jesus, my Lord, became man to take up my sins and my sinfulness in His own sinless humanity and to bury it all in His perfect death. He embraced me on His cross, and in Him I already am judged and crucified. Grant me to trust this with all my heart!

I dare not plead my good works before You, for they are hopelessly tarnished with sin. I do not plead my piety, nor even the depth of knowledge You have given me from the Holy Scriptures. I plead only the blood of Jesus Christ, Your Lamb who took away the sin of the world. I stand before You clothed only with His righteousness, innocence, and blessedness. He is my Rock; on Him I rest. He is my Redeemer; in Him I am hidden in safety.

I thank You, gracious Lord, for my Baptism. With

Your hand and in Your name, You buried me in the death of Your Son. You raised me in His resurrection. You seated me with Him at Your right hand in glory. You made me Your beloved child and opened heaven to me, washing away all my sin. You gave me Your own testimony, that I can face my death with a clear conscience, through the merits of Jesus, my Savior. And You did all this long before I knew even to ask for it. By grace I am saved!

I thank You for the gift of Absolution, those precious words calling out to me, forgiving me, reminding me, urging me to trust Your promises. I thank You for faithful pastors who preached the Word of forgiveness to me. I thank You for the company of the saints, my fellow pilgrims in Your holy Church—for their encouragements, their prayers, their works of mercy, their examples of faithfulness.

I thank You for the body and the blood of Your Son, Jesus Christ, my Lord. I go to His holy Supper as though I were going to my own death, so that I might go to my death as though going to His holy Supper. Surely, my cup overflows with mercy, and I can depart in peace, according to Your Word.

O Father in heaven, let Your name be hallowed in my death. Grant me to honor You in my dying breath, not that I may earn Your favor, but that those around me, whom I love and for whom Your Son has died, might also fear and trust in You.

Let Your kingdom come, that I may see You face-to-face, and live eternally under the reign of Jesus Christ, my Lord who died for me.

Let Your good and gracious will be done with me. Hinder and put to death the will of the devil, who would plague me with doubt and disbelief; the world, that would lead me to despair; and my own sinful flesh, that would drive me into myself and away from You.

Comfort those around me—my family, my friends, my neighbors, my doctors and nurses and all who care for me, my coworkers, my congregation and pastors. Bless them with Your strength in this time of trial. Remind them that You are the God of the living, whose Son conquered death by His dying and rising. Set the joy of Easter and the open, empty tomb of Jesus before their eyes, and wipe away every tear of grief. Encourage them with the knowledge that those who die in the Lord are not lost, nor are they far away, but they are as near as the Lord Jesus Christ, in whom live all the saints, joined together as one body, as we will see with our own eyes on the Day of Resurrection. Amen. (176)

Teach me to live that I may dread
The grave as little as my bed.
Teach me to die that so I may
Rise glorious at the awe-full day.
(*LSB* 883:3)

FOR A BLESSED END

O dear God and Lord! I live, yet I know not how long. I must die and yet I do not know when. But as You alone know, then, O Lord, my heavenly Father, let it be so! Should this day (this night) be the last of my life, Lord, Your will be done, for it alone is the best way. Therefore, I am ready to live and die in true faith in Christ, my Redeemer. Yet grant me but this plea, that I do not die suddenly in my sins. Give me a properly created knowledge, repentance, and sorrow concerning the sins that I have committed. Show them clearly to me in this life, that they might not be shown clearly on the Day of Judgment, and that because of that, I would go forth to everlasting shame before the sight of angels and of all people. O merciful Father, do not forsake me and take not Your Holy Spirit from me. Give me enough time and space for repentance that I may acknowledge and confess the transgressions of my heart, that I may obtain forgiveness and comfort from Your saving Word, and that I may be preserved for eternal life. O Lord, who knows all hearts, my heart yearns for its future with You; let me die when You so will. Yet, insofar as it is possible, grant me a reasonable, quiet, and blessed end.

O God, be gracious and merciful to me, a poor sinner. Amen. (177)

Lord Jesus Christ, the highest good,
You I implore through Your dear blood,
Just make my final hour good!

Selected Psalms

PSALM 23

1The LORD is my shepherd; I shall not want. 2He makes me lie down in green pastures. He leads me beside still waters. 3He restores my soul. He leads me in paths of righteousness for His name's sake.

4Even though I walk through the valley of the shadow of death, I will fear no evil, for You are with me; Your rod and Your staff, they comfort me.

5You prepare a table before me in the presence of my enemies; You anoint my head with oil; my cup overflows. 6Surely goodness and mercy shall follow me all the days of my life, and I shall dwell in the house of the LORD forever.

PSALM 32

1Blessed is the one whose transgression is forgiven, whose sin is covered. 2Blessed is the man against whom the LORD counts no iniquity, and in whose spirit there is no deceit.

3For when I kept silent, my bones wasted away
through my groaning all day long. 4For day and
night Your hand was heavy upon me; my strength
was dried up as by the heat of summer.

5I acknowledged my sin to You, and I did
not cover my iniquity; I said, "I will confess my
transgressions to the LORD," and You forgave the
iniquity of my sin.

6Therefore let everyone who is godly offer
prayer to You at a time when You may be found;
surely in the rush of great waters, they shall not
reach him. 7You are a hiding place for me; You
preserve me from trouble; You surround me with
shouts of deliverance.

8I will instruct you and teach you in the way
you should go; I will counsel you with My eye
upon you. 9Be not like a horse or a mule, without
understanding, which must be curbed with bit and
bridle, or it will not stay near you.

10Many are the sorrows of the wicked, but
steadfast love surrounds the one who trusts in
the LORD. 11Be glad in the LORD, and rejoice, O
righteous, and shout for joy, all you upright in heart!

PSALM
42

1As a deer pants for flowing streams, so pants
my soul for You, O God. 2My soul thirsts for God,
for the living God. When shall I come and appear
before God? 3My tears have been my food day and
night, while they say to me continually, "Where is
your God?" 4These things I remember, as I pour out
my soul: how I would go with the throng and lead
them in procession to the house of God with glad
shouts and songs of praise, a multitude keeping
festival.

5Why are you cast down, O my soul, and why
are you in turmoil within me? Hope in God; for I
shall again praise Him, my salvation 6and my God.

My soul is cast down within me; therefore I
remember You from the land of Jordan and of
Hermon, from Mount Mizar. 7Deep calls to deep
at the roar of Your waterfalls; all Your breakers
and Your waves have gone over me. 8By day the
LORD commands His steadfast love, and at night His
song is with me, a prayer to the God of my life. 9I
say to God, my rock: "Why have You forgotten me?

Why do I go mourning because of the oppression of the enemy?" [10]As with a deadly wound in my bones, my adversaries taunt me, while they say to me continually, "Where is your God?"

[11]Why are you cast down, O my soul, and why are you in turmoil within me? Hope in God; for I shall again praise Him, my salvation and my God.

PSALM 46

[1]God is our refuge and strength, a very present help in trouble. [2]Therefore we will not fear though the earth gives way, though the mountains be moved into the heart of the sea, [3]though its waters roar and foam, though the mountains tremble at its swelling.

[4]There is a river whose streams make glad the city of God, the holy habitation of the Most High. [5]God is in the midst of her; she shall not be moved; God will help her when morning dawns. [6]The nations rage, the kingdoms totter; He utters His voice, the earth melts. [7]The LORD of hosts is with us; the God of Jacob is our fortress.

[8]Come, behold the works of the LORD, how He has brought desolations on the earth. [9]He makes wars cease to the end of the earth; He breaks the bow and shatters the spear; He burns the chariots with fire.

[10]"Be still, and know that I am God. I will be exalted among the nations, I will be exalted in the earth!" [11]The LORD of hosts is with us; the God of Jacob is our fortress.

PSALM 51

[1]Have mercy on me, O God, according to Your steadfast love; according to Your abundant mercy blot out my transgressions. [2]Wash me thoroughly from my iniquity, and cleanse me from my sin!

[3]For I know my transgressions, and my sin is ever before me. [4]Against You, You only, have I sinned and done what is evil in Your sight, so that You may be justified in Your words and blameless in Your judgment. [5]Behold, I was brought forth in iniquity, and in sin did my mother conceive me. [6]Behold, You

delight in truth in the inward being, and You teach
me wisdom in the secret heart.

7Purge me with hyssop, and I shall be clean;
wash me, and I shall be whiter than snow. 8Let me
hear joy and gladness; let the bones that You have
broken rejoice. 9Hide Your face from my sins, and
blot out all my iniquities. 10Create in me a clean
heart, O God, and renew a right spirit within me.
11Cast me not away from Your presence, and take not
Your Holy Spirit from me. 12Restore to me the joy of
Your salvation, and uphold me with a willing spirit.

13Then I will teach transgressors Your ways,
and sinners will return to You. 14Deliver me from
bloodguiltiness, O God, O God of my salvation,
and my tongue will sing aloud of Your righteousness.
15O Lord, open my lips, and my mouth will declare
Your praise. 16For You will not delight in sacrifice,
or I would give it; You will not be pleased with a
burnt offering. 17The sacrifices of God are a broken
spirit; a broken and contrite heart, O God, You will
not despise.

18Do good to Zion in Your good pleasure; build
up the walls of Jerusalem; 19then will You delight in
right sacrifices, in burnt offerings and whole burnt
offerings; then bulls will be offered on Your altar.

PSALM
63:1–8

1 O God, You are my God; earnestly I seek You;
my soul thirsts for You; my flesh faints for You,
as in a dry and weary land where there is no water.
2 So I have looked upon You in the sanctuary,
beholding Your power and glory. 3 Because Your
steadfast love is better than life, my lips will praise
You. 4 So I will bless You as long as I live; in Your
name I will lift up my hands.

5 My soul will be satisfied as with fat and rich
food, and my mouth will praise You with joyful lips,
6 when I remember You upon my bed, and meditate
on You in the watches of the night; 7 for You have
been my help, and in the shadow of Your wings
I will sing for joy. 8 My soul clings to You; Your right
hand upholds me.

PSALM

121

1 I lift up my eyes to the hills. From where does
my help come? 2 My help comes from the LORD, who
made heaven and earth.

3 He will not let your foot be moved; He who
keeps you will not slumber. 4 Behold, He who keeps
Israel will neither slumber nor sleep.

5 The LORD is your keeper; the LORD is your
shade on your right hand. 6 The sun shall not strike
you by day, nor the moon by night.

7 The LORD will keep you from all evil; He will
keep your life. 8 The LORD will keep your going out
and your coming in from this time forth and
forevermore.

PSALM
130

1Out of the depths I cry to You, O LORD!
2O Lord, hear my voice! Let Your ears be attentive
to the voice of my pleas for mercy!

3If You, O LORD, should mark iniquities, O Lord,
who could stand? 4But with You there is forgiveness,
that You may be feared.

5I wait for the LORD, my soul waits, and in His
word I hope; 6my soul waits for the Lord more than
watchmen for the morning, more than watchmen
for the morning.

7O Israel, hope in the LORD! For with the LORD
there is steadfast love, and with Him is plentiful
redemption. 8And He will redeem Israel from all
his iniquities.

Suggestions as to Other Psalms

Psalms of Praise and Thanksgiving	103, 144–150
Psalms for Periods of Distress	6, 28, 38, 77
Psalms for Times of Illness	39, 65, 71, 90, 91
Psalms for Times of Spiritual Affliction	73, 126
Psalms Pertaining to the Spreading of the Church	87, 97
Psalms Asking Blessings upon Divine Worship	27, 100, 122
Psalms Exalting Christ and His Work	2, 22, 45, 110
Psalms Asking for the Strengthening of Faith	34, 118, 139
Psalms for Those Discouraged	25, 40, 86
Psalms for Convalescents	84, 116, 138

THE NICENE CREED

I believe in one God, the Father Almighty, maker of heaven and earth and of all things visible and invisible.

And in one Lord Jesus Christ, the only-begotten Son of God, begotten of His Father before all worlds, God of God, Light of Light, very God of very God, begotten, not made, being of one substance with the Father, by whom all things were made; who for us men and for our salvation came down from heaven and was incarnate by the Holy Spirit of the Virgin Mary and was made man; and was crucified also for us under Pontius Pilate. He suffered and was buried. And the third day He rose again according to the Scriptures and ascended into heaven and sits at the right hand of the Father. And He will come again with glory to judge both the living and the dead, whose kingdom will have no end.

And I believe in the Holy Spirit, the Lord and giver of life, who proceeds from the Father and the Son, who with the Father and the Son together is worshiped and glorified, who spoke by the prophets. And I believe in one holy Christian and apostolic Church,

I acknowledge one Baptism for the remission of sins, and I look for the resurrection of the dead and the life of the world to come. Amen.

THE ATHANASIAN CREED

Whoever will be saved shall, above all else, hold the catholic faith. Which faith, except everyone keeps whole and undefiled, without doubt he will perish eternally.

And the catholic faith is this, that we worship one God in three persons and three persons in one God, neither confusing the persons nor dividing the substance. For there is one person of the Father, another of the Son, and another of the Holy Spirit. But the Godhead of the Father, of the Son, and of the Holy Spirit is all one: the glory equal, the majesty coeternal. Such as the Father is, such is the Son, and such is the Holy Spirit. The Father uncreated, the Son uncreated, and the Holy Spirit uncreated. The Father incomprehensible, the Son incomprehensible, and the Holy Spirit incomprehensible. The Father eternal, the Son eternal, and the Holy Spirit eternal. And yet They are not three eternals but one eternal. As there are not three uncreated nor three incomprehensibles but one uncreated and one incomprehensible. So likewise the Father is almighty, the Son almighty, and the Holy Spirit almighty. And yet They are not three almighties but one almighty. So the Father is God, the Son is God, and the Holy Spirit is God. And yet They are not three Gods but one God. So likewise the Father is Lord, the Son Lord, and the Holy Spirit Lord. And yet They are not three Lords but one Lord. For as we are compelled by the Christian truth to acknowledge every person by Himself to be both God and Lord, so we cannot by the catholic faith say that there are three Gods or three Lords. The Father is made of none, neither created nor begotten. The Son is of the Father alone, not made nor created but begotten. The Holy Spirit is of the Father and of the Son, neither made nor created nor begotten but proceeding. So there is one Father, not three Fathers; one Son, not three Sons; one Holy Spirit, not three Holy Spirits. And in this Trinity none is before or after another; none is greater or less than another; but the whole three persons are coeternal together and coequal, so that in all things, as is aforesaid, the Unity in Trinity and the Trinity in Unity is to be worshiped.

He, therefore, that will be saved is compelled thus to think of the Trinity. Furthermore, it is necessary to everlasting salvation that he also believe faithfully the incarnation of our Lord Jesus Christ. For the right faith is that we believe and confess that our Lord Jesus Christ, the Son of God, is God and man; God of the substance of the Father, begotten before the worlds; and man of the substance of His mother, born in the world; perfect God and perfect man, of a reasonable soul and human flesh subsisting. Equal to the Father as touching His Godhead and inferior to the Father as touching His manhood; who, although He is God and man, yet He is not two but one Christ: One, not by conversion of the Godhead into flesh but by taking the manhood into God; one altogether, not by confusion of substance but by unity of person. For as the reasonable soul and flesh is one man, so God and man is one Christ; who suffered for our salvation, descended into hell, rose again the third day from the dead. He ascended into heaven, He sits at the right hand of the Father, God Almighty, from whence He will come to judge the living and the dead. At whose coming all men will rise again with their bodies and will give an account of their own works. And they that have done good will go into life everlasting; and they that have done evil, into everlasting fire.

This is the catholic faith which, except a man believe faithfully and firmly, he cannot be saved. Amen.

Index

ISBN 978-0-7586-8232-1
9 780758 682321
RELIGION/Christian Living/
Prayer **061334**